Village Greens of New England

LEXINGTON GREEN is *the* green, the most typical and symbolic one of all.

VILLAGE GREENS OF NEW ENGLAND

Louise Andrews Kent

PHOTOGRAPHS BY

Arthur Griffin

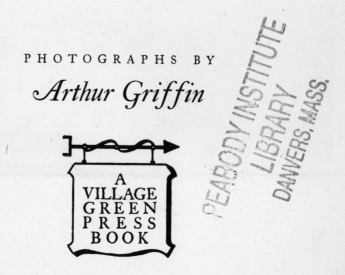

A VILLAGE GREEN PRESS BOOK

M. BARROWS & COMPANY, INC., NEW YORK

F
5
K4

917.4

K37

For S. H. L.

Who Used to Like Driving Through New England

Acknowledgments

The W. P. A. Guides to the six New England States, published by the Houghton Mifflin Company, were indispensable in laying the groundwork for this study of New England's village greens and commons. Many town histories also were used of which some of the most helpful were those of Billerica, Brookline, Lancaster, Leominster, and Royalston in Massachusetts; Durham, New 'Hampshire; Wiscasset, Maine; and New Haven, Connecticut. Valuable material, not elsewhere available, was found in James Duncan Phillips' splendid series of books on Salem—especially *Salem in the Eighteenth Century*—and in Mrs. Caleb Wheeler's collection of information on old Concord houses. I found this in the Public Library of Concord, Massachusetts.

The author is grateful to Miss Florence Wheeler of the Leominster Public Library for her friendly interest and encouragement; to the owner of the Wheeler House at Orford, New Hampshire, for facts about the houses on "The Ridge"; to Mrs. Thomas Groom for drawing our attention to the great variety of transitions in New England church steeples; to Mr. and Mrs. Jarvis Hadley for discovering Royalston Common and insisting that the author visit it; to

[7]

Mrs. Theodore Dillon for perceiving the unique quality of the Tabernacle Green on Martha's Vineyard; to Mrs. Thaddeus Defriez II, for her patience while the author copied inscriptions from old tombstones and vanished for indefinite periods into libraries, and especially to Helen Van Pelt Wilson for supplying the idea of the book in the first place and for her painstaking editorial assistance.

FOREWORD

Elm-Shaded Is Not Enough

It was a remark made by Henry James in *The American Scene* that set us wondering about the village greens and old commons of New England. James suggested that when you described a village as "elm-shaded," you had said so much that little else remained. He went on, however, to discuss various aspects of the villages—their neatness, grassy margins, fresh white paint, open dooryards, great feathery arches of elms, and the impression of houses both sunned and shaded. It troubled him that, though the items were so few, they added up to a sum so much greater than the separate parts seemed capable of producing.

James did not linger over this puzzle. He called himself a restless analyst and, after a patronizing glance at white houses set around sun-dappled greens, apparently chose to be more restless than analytical. He said he would not on any account come back in winter when the white paint would be dingy against the snow. It struck us then that his sum did not add up right because he was not aware of all the parts.

The green oasis under the elms, which is the heart of so many New England towns, is perhaps most characteristic when the impression is of cool green and white, but you

1. DEERFIELD, MASSACHUSETTS. The village takes on new life in the months of naked glare.

[10]

must know it, too, in what James called the months of naked glare. Far from looking dingy, as he supposed, the village in winter takes on new life and color. The Gothic thrust of elms against the sky is no longer hidden by thick foliage. Instead there is the intricate tracery of twigs and branches, shifting in tone from gray or brown to misty purple. After fresh snow the trees are black and white etchings. Every twig, every roughness of bark is sharply accented. If the snow melts and freezes again, the morning sun shines on branches encased in rainbows.

Color overlooked when the leaves were green is emphasized now—the warm tones of old brick chimneys and red barns, scarlet sleds pulled by little girls in red snow suits, an Irish setter with snow on his silky henna-colored coat, pink geraniums in sunny windows. In winter, it is noticeable that all New Englanders do not paint their houses white. Some unconforming families choose yellow and stick to it for a hundred years. When the trees are bare, it brings new warmth to the landscape. So do polished brass doorknobs and eagle knockers, the shining cap on the meetinghouse steeple and gold horses prancing on weather vanes.

There is plenty of blue, too. Changes in the sky are more visible in winter than in summer and they bring out the green-faded-to-blue of old shutters and doors. Still the most brilliant blue is not in light but in shade. Under the edge of every clapboard and cornice, outlining the trellises and the bare vines on them, following the paths of sleds or ploughs or feet in overshoes, recording the swaying of the elms, or the tail feathers of a pheasant, is a blue shadow. To remember this in midsummer is to add to your column of impressions. The sum begins to come out better. It will be closer to balancing if you know the village, too, when there are bronze flowers on the elms and in the dooryards, daffodils swing in a sharp spring wind. A little later, when the leaves are the size of squirrels' ears, there will be the orange flash of orioles among them, fire hangbirds, the boys call them, because of their knitted, gray-pocket nests.

Spring moves at a quiet pace when it reaches old commons. A warm day brings out spires of carved ivory on white lilacs and scarlet buds on apple trees. Then a wind blows down from the icebergs near Labrador and you must wait a week for the flowering and remember that Ralph Waldo Emerson said of the New England spring, "Some survive it." While you wait, the forsythia which should have gone long ago remains a cascade of gold. Cherry blossoms last as if they were made of crêpe paper and the emerald shine of the grass on the village green is blinding.

To let "elm-shaded" cover the look of New England is to be unaware of blossoms on red maples, the lighted candles of new pine growth, and the pink and silver of young oak leaves. It is to forget the changes autumn brings when the white houses have a different look because the elms above them are yellow instead of green. Then wood smoke rises blue out of chimneys. There are orange pumpkins on doorsteps, rows of red and yellow tomatoes ripening on windowsills, and purple berries gleaming among scarlet woodbine leaves. Blue birds are bits of sky on the wing. On frosty nights Orion sparkles above a hill that may be covered with snow by morning.

No, "elm-shaded" is not enough.

Yet these elms around the greens are worth considering. Fifty years is nothing in the life of such trees. The one here at our window was planted more than half a century ago. Yet it is only six feet in girth, measured five feet above the ground. Oliver Wendell Holmes, who called them his tree brides and wore out a measuring tape on elms, discovered some more than twenty feet in circumference and with a hundred feet of spread. Holmes considered the Old Elm on Boston Common, which was there when the first settlers came, a tree of only the second class. Like the other giants he knew, it was not planted but grew in a place of its own choosing.

The elms we see shading New England greens today were set out, not scattered accidentally. Who planted them and laid out the greens they shade, and for what purpose? Why is one space called a green and another a common? Who keeps the grass mowed and the fences painted? Why are some towns planned around a central green and others along a main street? Must greens always be level and of prescribed shape? What were the greens used for when the first houses were built near them? What are they used for now? How long has the white meetinghouse stood with its spire rising among the elms and why is there so often a tavern near it? What kind of people lived in the houses with the fanlighted doors?

Perhaps in the answers to these questions we will discover the reason the total impression made by a New England village is stronger than the separate facts seem to warrant. Perhaps from the answers we may also understand something of what lies behind the white fences and the lovely fluted columns.

It will be well worth trying.

January, 1948   *Louise Andrews Kent*
Brookline
Massachusetts

Contents

Illustrations

Village Greens of New England

CHAPTER *I*

Is It Green or Common?

*E*very one of us who knows New England has in mind some picture of a village green. Perhaps we know one intimately and each of its features seems necessary. This we consider the true green, all others are imitations. Perhaps we know many greens superficially and have constructed a mental kaleidoscope in which Ionic porticoes, elms, bandstands, honor rolls, white steeples, tavern signs, small-paned windows, and green turf can be shaken into an infinite number of attractive patterns. Whatever our picture, it is almost certainly right in many ways.

Yet any assertion about village greens needs to be qualified. Usually they are triangular, but at Weston in Vermont the green is circular with a small green triangle lying just outside it, and a crescent, too—grassy islands cut away from the central common by diverging roads. At Rutland, the green on Main Street is a long slender oblong, so long that it is almost a mall. Woodstock's lovely old houses face a narrow maple-shaded oval. Although elms seem essential, on these three greens, maples flower in spring and flame in fall. In most pictures all the houses are white, but Woodstock surprises us with rose-pink brick and stone shading from cream to topaz, and when we look expectantly for a white fence, we are startled by something of peculiar ugliness in green painted iron.

In old records we have often read that greens are common property maintained by the towns. Then we find that at Haverhill Corner, New Hampshire, the common belongs to the proprietors whose houses face on it and that it is kept up by them. It is no more common property—as we usually understand the term—than is Louisburg Square in Boston, which is also maintained by proprietors, not by the city. This Square has statues, yet they mark no heroism in war but are said to have been brought as ballast in a ship and set up there because, with true New England economy, it seemed too bad to waste them. So Aristides guards one end of the Square and Columbus the other, and the proprietors see that both are well scrubbed.

Is Louisburg Square a village green? It has the air of serenity, white doorways, the sense of both sun and shade, of being at the same time exclusive and neighborly, of remaining changeless in a changing world. These contradictions are the right ones. A village green is always partly in the world and partly separated from it. Even the proprietors of Louisburg Square telephone the police if they find the cars of foreigners from Waltham or Cambridge parked at their doors and on Christmas Eve, when the windows are shining with candles, when snow is sifting down on the lighted trees, when carols are sung and the mingled fragrance of fir balsam, rum punch, and toasted cheese drifts out of open doors, the Square is no more private than the North Station when a ski train is departing.

How then shall we define a village green? We might, we suppose, find justification for giving the name to any open green space jointly owned by a town, a city, or a group of individuals. Perhaps we cannot come much closer than that.

As we drive through New England, we find that greens vary greatly in size. What was once a wide common may have been pared down to a weedy triangle hardly large enough to contain the Honor Roll of the Second World

2. HARDWICK, MASSACHUSETTS.   It seems as if a town could develop in
no other way.

[25]

War. Some greens, however, have been protected by public-spirited citizens who have fought to preserve them against the encroachments of progress so that like New Haven Green or Boston Common, they still keep something of their old spaciousness. Sometimes the charm of a green lies not in its extent but in its compactness as in the one at Grafton, Massachusetts. Seen in the summer twilight, Grafton appears the natural setting for a New England story, so the visitor is not surprised to learn that it was the background for the filming of Eugene O'Neill's *Ah, Wilderness!*

There is an inevitable quality about such greens: they should be as they are and where they are. A town could develop, it seems, in no other way. Having reached this conclusion, we discover that the next town has been built along a main street. These main-street towns, however, are usually more recent developments than those which grew up around central commons. For instance, in Dedham, Massachusetts, the eighteenth-century houses face a wide common, one of the pleasantest in New England, while Norwood, once a part of Dedham but settled later, arranges itself along a main street. Then there are the towns which grew where main roads crossed.

All this makes us wonder if the pattern of a town is not after all rather accidental. As we study the records of different towns, it seems so. Certainly the early settlers did not visualize the greens as we see them today. They apparently developed because they were necessary to the life of the settlement. Too often they disappeared when the practical need for them passed.

Old records reveal also that there was little distinction between greens and commons. According to Mr. Webster's best-seller, "a common is a place for pleasure, for pasturage." We would like to believe that pleasure was the idea behind these elm-shaded green spaces—there are literally hundreds of them in New England—but we fear our ancestors were thinking mainly of pasturage. Except perhaps Thomas Morton, who laid out the most authentically English of all New

England village greens at Mount Wollaston now part of Quincy. He called his settlement Merrymount and, to the horror of his Puritan neighbors, set up a maypole, taught the Indians to dance around it, and, in defiance of royal edict, supplied them with rum and with firearms so that they could kill game for him. Sometimes he called his town Maremont, Hill by the Sea, for he could make a Latin pun. Finally the Puritans, who had several reasons for disapproving of him, seized Thomas Morton and shipped him back to England and it was a long time before there was dancing again on any New England greens. Pasturage not pleasure, we realized regretfully, was the compelling motive in their development.

Returning to our dictionary, we find a green defined as "a common, as a village green." A common, then, is not necessarily a green, although a green is always a common. Common is the larger term and may mean only rough, rocky, upland pasture with no houses near it at all. A green is the center of a community. It may be called a common but still it has about it a feeling of compactness, of neighborliness that belongs to the time when small towns were self-sufficing, weaving wool shorn from their own sheep, grinding their own grain, baking bricks for the occasional mansion house that accents the green and white pattern of the village, making their own harness and saddles from the hides of their own steers.

Local craftsmen built the houses around the greens. Glass for the small-paned windows and for the fanlights over the doors came from a distance, but the timbers and clapboards, shingles and panels once grew on hillsides above the town. The brook with its blue flags and jewelweed supplied the power that sawed the boards. The village blacksmith hammered out hinges and latches. If nails were needed, he made them, but many of the old houses were joined almost entirely with wooden pegs. It is natural enough that the houses look as if they grew out of the ground on which they stand. For the most part they did.

Those days when the blacksmith would finish shoeing a horse and then set to work on a strap hinge for somebody's barn door are gone long ago. The door where the hinge still swings is a century old or more. The common is often much older and the underlying reason for its existence may be traced back a thousand years before it gets lost in the mists of antiquity. The English settlers, who came first to Plymouth and a few years later to Salem and Boston, brought with them ideas about the ownership of land that were already old in England when William the Conqueror crossed the channel. The system of agriculture, based on these ideas, came into England with the Angles and Saxons. It was called the common field system. The historian, Tacitus, found German tribes carrying on farming in this way which goes back to the time when nomads settled down and had to plan for a fair division of land. First the division was among members of a family; then, as the group increased, between members of a clan, later among neighbors.

There is a record of how in 1500 twelve elders of a village organized a community. They began by laying out a village green, which was in the center of the town and was to be used as a night pasture to protect cattle from wolves and thieves. The rest of the land was divided into plough land, meadow land, and common. Each householder was assigned a piece of plough land near his house for an orchard. His meadows might be at some distance away. Each holding contained some of the better land and some of the poorer. Sometimes things were equalized by assigning a larger amount of the poorer land to one owner.

The common land belonged to the whole village and all the landholders had certain rights in it. They could lop off the limbs for their own firewood, but not cut down trees and go into the lumber business. They could dig up gravel or clay for their own use but not sell it. They had the right of turbary, the cutting of turf for fuel. This fuel might consist of a gorse bush, roots and all, and the turf that came with it— a backbreaking and prickly privilege. Villagers could remove grass from the common land but only "by the mouths of their cattle"; they could not store it or sell it.

If you have in your china cupboard a blue Staffordshire plate bordered with seashells or roses and showing Boston State House and some placid cows, removing, or having recently removed, grass by their mouths from the Common, you have an early nineteenth-century assertion of one of these ancient rights. Indeed, only the other day we saw a lovely, cream-colored Jersey being milked on Boston Common. Were she and her calf, an innocent looking creature as pretty as a young fawn, driven to the Common along the old right of way leading from Beacon Hill by which Benjamin Franklin and later Ralph Waldo Emerson used to drive the family cows? We like to think so, although, as this event occurred in National Dairy Week, we have an uneasy feeling that more likely the visitors arrived on the Charles Street side and in a truck.

On the common, cattle were more easily protected from wolves. Wolves were a danger to the early settlements and so were Indians. Even the friendly Indians sometimes found it easier to hunt beef than venison. The earliest settlements were often enclosed by a stockade behind which animals as well as owners could be safe from Indian attacks. Our grandmother used to tell us a story, told her by her great grandmother, about a small girl, Hepzibah Gray, who lived in a lonely, seventeenth-century settlement west of Boston. It consisted of a few houses clustered together and fenced away from the shadowy wilderness where at night a cry might be the howling of a wolf, the scream of a catamount, or an Indian war whoop. When darkness came, the only light was from rushes dipped in grease or from the logs burning in the fire place. Brick chimneys were a luxury then for many of these early houses had chimneys of wood daubed with clay. The Gray's house had a brick chimney and also glass in its diamond-paned windows. Hepzibah liked to look through them and watch for her father and the other men of the village to come home from their work in the fields outside. Her big brother would be driving the brindled cow back to the night pasture and her father, with his gun over his shoulder, tired from ploughing all day, would be walking beside the oxen.

Sometimes her father went hunting and the oxen would be tethered outside on the common. It could hardly be called a green yet. There were still stumps of trees on it and although there was grass, there were weeds too—golden rod, asters, ferns, joe-pye weed. Where the brush had been piled there were raspberries growing up. There were blackberries, too. Hepzibah had picked some that day and was saving the biggest and shiniest ones for her father. He was out hunting and he might bring back a wild turkey. Hepzibah knew just how it would look with the sun shining on the bronze feathers. She knew a good deal about her world although, in spite of being four years old, she did not talk plainly. Indeed she preferred not to talk at all. The mothers of more loquacious daughters pitied Mrs. Gray for having such a backward child.

On this September day the maples had already begun to turn and Hepzibah was watching the path under the flame and orange branches. Once she thought she saw some one move along it. She pushed open the casement to see better but the path was empty. Her mother was making soft soap in a wooden bucket, stirring it with a long paddle cut from a piece of pine. Hepzibah wrinkled her small nose and leaned farther out the window. The smell of soap was not one she liked.

This time she was sure she saw something move in the maples beyond the raspberry patch. She heard a noise—only a rustle, hardly more than a robin makes leaving its nest. Then something rose out of the brush pile: first some feathers, then some greasy black hair and below it a face streaked with red and black paint, with a red and black band around the mouth making it look enormous.

Hepzibah got down off the bench she had been standing on and tugged at her mother's skirt.

"Him top fevvers, him head, him ugly mouf," she said.

Her mother did not understand.

"Go and watch for father. He'll come soon," she said.

Hepzibah went back to the window and watched the brush pile. Perhaps the varmint—that was what she had heard her father call Indians—had gone away, but he hadn't. This time she saw two of them—feathers, black hair, hideously smeared faces and all, rise again out of the brush, only nearer, almost at the house. She ran to her mother again and tugged hard at her skirt.

"Two top fevvers, two ugly mouf," she said.

Still her mother did not understand her.

"Two *varmints*," the little girl gasped out, driven to speaking plainly.

Her mother lifted the heavy bucket of soap and moved quietly to the window as the feathers rose above the sill and after them the red and black faces and the terrible mouths. Hepzibah saw her mother swing the bucket, saw the golden stream of hot soap fly through the air. There were screams, worse than the yelling of panthers, as the Indians crashed through the brush, scrambled over the fence, and ran off into the woods. Ezekiel Gray heard them as he came home with a turkey over his shoulder. He came running through the asters to the door, thumped on it, calling, until his wife unbarred it.

They told him the story, she and Hepzibah. He told it to every one in the settlement—until people got pretty tired of hearing it, our grandmother said—and he always ended up, "I want you should know that Hepzibah can talk as plain as anyone when she's a mind to."

Rights of pasturage used to belong to certain houses in America just as they did in England. We like to imagine the present residents of Beacon Street in the section opposite Boston Common driving cows to pasture, lopping off branches (estovers), bringing in wood (firebote), and cutting turf. Unfortunately for this dream, the city took away these rights many years ago so there is no use renting an apartment today in one of those houses with violet glass-windows so as to pasture your cow across the street! In fact, commons and greens are seldom places for pasturage now, but they are still used for pleasure, a pleasure which they offer to every visitor willing to turn aside from main roads and rest a while under their elms. The roots of so many Americans are in these peaceful village commons that they bring to us not only a sense of dignity, serenity, and quiet beauty, but also of home-coming.

CHAPTER 2

The Meetinghouse, Vital Center of a Town

*M*émories of village greens naturally center around an
old meetinghouse with a white steeple. Until the
nineteenth century, church and town were closely linked and
the meetinghouse was just what it was called, a house in
which members of the community met to decide about all
manner of things—the building of roads, the buying of land
from the Indians, the kind of clothes women might wear, or
who was to be put in the stocks. In the meetinghouse also
were delivered the terrible lectures on infant damnation and
original sin. Indeed no building was so vitally necessary to
the development of a town.

To own land in Massachusetts a settler first had to convince the authorities of his religious orthodoxy. The privilege of citizenship was difficult to win and easy to lose.
Rhode Island and Connecticut were both settled by men too
liberal for Massachusetts. They left it, sometimes forcibly
exiled, sometimes of their own free will.

The buildings where the first settlers met were not the
white meetinghouses we know. The tablet that marks the
First Church of a community also frequently indicates that

this is the third or fourth building to bear that name. Often it is the most beautiful of the successive structures. If it was built in the late eighteenth or the early nineteenth century, there is probably somewhere in its history a design by Sir Christopher Wren. In fact, we have heard it said that, since so many of his English churches were bombed, the best place to look for Wren's work is in New England.

In many cases, after country carpenters have adapted designs from brick and stone to wood and after one church had been copied from another, it is difficult to trace the influence exactly. Yet it is easy to sense it in such churches as the one on Ashby Green in Massachusetts. There the triple doorway, the delicate detail of the cornice, the fine proportions of the bell tower, and the well-placed windows combine to make this one of the most satisfying of New England meetinghouses. Perhaps the best time to visit Ashby is late in spring. All through the surrounding region, apple orchards are in bloom in May, and following them, the woods are filled with the pink and white shell-like blossoms of the mountain laurel. Still when we traveled through this part of Massachusetts in September and could smell the ripening apples before we saw the trees laden with scarlet fruit, and the woods around us were a brilliant panorama of crimson and gold and burnt orange, we wondered if Ashby were not loveliest of all in the autumn.

Another beautiful meetinghouse rises beside the common at Groton. Built in 1755, it was later carefully restored to preserve the appearance and feeling of an eighteenth-century church. A Paul Revere bell hangs in the belfry below the gold-cock weather vane and the spire is well-designed. Groton meetinghouse has long been a landmark in war as well as in peace for it presides over a common which was a training ground for Revolutionary soldiers and the place of meeting for the men who marched to Concord and Lexington on the morning of the nineteenth of April, 1775.

The steeples of New England meetinghouses are a study in themselves. The men who built them, whether or not

3. ASHBY, MASSACHUSETTS. Somewhere in this church's history there is
probably a design by Sir Christopher Wren.

[35]

4. (*Opposite*) PARK STREET CHURCH, BOSTON. The steeples of New England meetinghouses are a study in themselves.

they carried a book of Wren's designs in their pockets, showed considerable ingenuity in achieving a transition from the square box at the base of the steeple to the eight-sided pepper pot at the top. If you look at a number of these spires, you will see that there is no set way of solving this problem. In fact, in the nineteenth century the builder often declined to notice that there was a problem and simply set the eight-sided spike on top of the box—with hideous results.

The steeple of Park Street Church on Boston Common, however, has been carefully contrived. The eye is gradually led upward from one stage to the next. It moves from the square clock tower to another square structure, each side of which resembles the entrance of a classic temple with columns and pediment; then to the first octagonal lantern, a more delicate structure than the preceding one; then to a similar but smaller one; again to a still smaller lantern, but this time with an oval window in each of the eight sides. Finally, there is the handsome hexagonal spire itself. Interest is caught and held by each of the changes and, in following them, you experience a soaring sensation which is never produced by the toothpick-on-box type of steeple.

Some steeples, you will notice, do not end in spires at all but are capped by small gold domes and surmounted by weather vanes. Here again the way of reaching the weather vane is never twice the same. The difference may be slight— a latticed window in one tower, an open arch in another, a railing here, quoins there—but in each case there will be something to show that the builder had his own idea of what a steeple should be.

5. BEDFORD, MASSACHUSETTS. Some steeples rush to the sky; others take
their time.

Some steeples rush to the sky; others take their time. In Bedford, Massachusetts, there is one of these deliberate designs of a kind we have seen nowhere else. The lower part of the tower is of such generous porportions that, from the front, the church appears to be a four-story building with a short tower. Actually the two upper rooms are in the steeple, which is of average height. The transition from square to octagonal is not made until the fifth stage. At this point there is a lantern topped by a domelike cap and a weather vane.

Another unusual steeple rises on the Congregational Church at Lyme, New Hampshire. Here no transition has been attempted. The tower is composed of three diminishing squares with an egg-shaped dome resting on the third one. A delicate railing surrounds each division of the steeple and the whole thing—clock faces, railings, pointed windows, dome, and weather vane—has something strongly individual about it. The domed top and pointed finials suggest oriental influence, yet the steeple seems quite at home with elms and maples and fanlighted doorways.

Above Templeton Green, in Massachusetts, the church steeple reaches a beautiful finality through five changing phases. The first is a closed box with clocks; the second stage is open; the third, octagonal with round-topped arches; the fourth is a lantern with oval windows. The spire itself is brief, but the whole effect is of a swift and sudden thrust toward the sky. And again the delicacy of the varied railings adds airy grace to the steeple, while the feeling of height is increased by pairs of slender Ionic pillars on the portico.

It was customary for the building committee of one town to copy the church of another. When the people of Calais, Vermont, set aside land for a meetinghouse and graveyard, Colonel Caleb Curtiss, one of the committee, went to Salisbury, Connecticut, and drew plans for the new church from the one there. We passed the Salisbury Church lately and stopped to trace the resemblance. It is there, although the Calais church resembles the Salisbury one only as a plain

6. LYME, NEW HAMPSHIRE. The domed top and pointed finials suggest oriental influence.

[40]

daughter sometimes resembles a beautiful mother. There is the same dignity and simplicity about both buildings and this is not at all dependent on surface ornamentation.

Perhaps the Old West Church in Calais retains its original appearance as much as any New England meetinghouse. It still shines outside with white paint. Inside, the pine of the old box pews has mellowed to brown in pleasant contrast to the smoke-blue paint of gallery and pulpit. The paint looks fresh, but it was put on in 1886. At the same time, this admonition was lettered above the pulpit, "Remove not the ancient landmark which thy fathers have set."

In looking at these old churches, even the simplest of them, and in the houses around village greens, we notice that up to about 1840 it seems to have been almost impossible to build a really ugly structure. Horse sheds with their arched openings, blacksmith shops, corn barns, ash houses, springhouses, sawmills, clapboard cottages, brick mansions with pillared porches—they all look right. Around 1840, ingenious machines were invented to save labor and after that whatever was built looks wrong. Even when an old church is exactly copied, something—it is difficult to say just what—produces a feeling of unreality in the new building. Perhaps it is the razoredges of wood baked dry and planed by machine or the flawless clarity of the glass, clear as an automobile windshield, or the undeviating bricks, baked efficiently by the thousand out of material mixed by formula, but certainly the various textures, only subtly different in any one way, fail to convince us that the building belongs in the eighteenth century. We feel instinctively that there is an oil burner in the basement, that the carpet is the best broadloom and cleaned with a vacuum cleaner, that the Women's Auxiliary never earned money to pay first for gas fixtures and then more money to have them taken out and electricity put in, that the organ never wheezed because some twelve-year-old boy was reading *Treasure Island* and forgot to pump. We sense all this, even as we drive quickly past.

Today we are so accustomed to seeing white meeting-

7. TEMPLETON, MASSACHUSETTS. The spire is brief, but the effect is a
swift and sudden thrust toward the sky.

houses all through New England that we forget how very different were the earliest places of worship. We know how the church at Salem must have looked because Nathaniel Hawthorne described it for us:

The central object was an edifice of humble architecture with neither bell nor steeple to proclaim what nevertheless it was—the house of prayer. A token of the perils of the wilderness was seen in the grim head of a wolf which had just been slain within the precincts of the town, and, according to the regular mode of claiming the bounty, was nailed to the porch of the meetinghouse. The blood was still plashing on the door-step.

In close vicinity to the sacred edifice appeared that important engine of Puritan authority, the whipping post—with the soil around it well trodden by the feet of evildoers who had there been disciplined. At one corner of the meetinghouse was a pillory, and at the other the stocks; the head of an Episcopalian and suspected Catholic was grotesquely incased in the former machine, while a fellow criminal, who had boisterously quaffed a health to the King, was confined by the legs in the latter.

Across from Salem on the opposite shore of Massachusetts Bay at Hingham is the only seventeenth-century meetinghouse still standing in New England. It is known as the Old Ship Church. It is on the main street of the town and the common land around it, on which there was once an old fort for protection against Indians, is now a graveyard. The church is said to have been built by ships' carpenters and the interior arrangement does suggest that of a ship. It was this Hingham church which was the inspiration for the design of the great seventeenth-century hall in the American Wing of the Metropolitan Museum in New York. The church is a severely plain structure on the outside. It has no spire. Instead a belfry with a lookout above it rises a short distance above the squared-off pyramid of the roof. From this lookout, anxious watch must often have been kept, for the church stood through some of the worst of the Indian wars.

Once a funeral sermon was preached at Hingham for a

Major Thaxter, who was supposed to have been killed by the Indians. The major got home to Hingham just too late to hear the sermon and met a friend coming away from the meetinghouse.

"Why, Major! What are you doing here?" exclaimed the friend. "We just buried you!"

When a meeting was to be held in one of these old churches the people were summoned by the sound of drums beaten on the common. Then a guard of young men with long guns over their shoulders followed the drummers across the green and waited while the minister and the rest of the company entered the meetinghouse. During the service, guards stood at the windows and at the door—in Hingham probably also in the lookout—to watch for hostile Indians. The houses of the village were empty and unprotected because everyone had to be present at meeting, even Quakers, who were unwelcome in the Puritan settlements. When we find a town without a central green, we sometimes discover that it was settled by Quakers, who did not level the land in front of their meetinghouses for training grounds. Attendance at Puritan meetings was no pleasure to the Quakers and the women sometimes showed their lack of sympathy with the proceedings by knitting through the sermon. The tithingman would try to stop them, but he had so much to attend to—tickling nodding women and snoring men with a squirrel's tail tied to the end of a stick, rapping wriggling boys and giggling girls over the head with the hard end, and preventing less-favored members from improving their social position by sneaking into the front seats—that sometimes the heel of a stocking would be finished in spite of his supervision!

Quakers were not alone in finding the Puritan service strange. Since all Indians were not hostile, friendly and curious ones sometimes would wander into the meetinghouse and squat down on the floor to observe the white man's antics and listen gravely to his nasal singing. There was no instrumental music. One of the elders "lined out" the hymn

—that is, he sang the first line and the congregation repeated it. Then he followed with the second and so they
worked through such favorites as:

> *Oh! What a thankless wretch was I*
> *To moan and mutter and repine*
> *To see the wicked placed on high*
> *In silken robes of honor shine!*

concluding happily with the statement that,

> *The fiery pit below them rolls.*

The punishment described by the hymns was not always
impersonal nor scheduled for the distant future. The minister meted out suitable and immediate correctives to parishioners whose frailties had been discovered during the week
just past. No doubt this was the pleasantest part of the
meeting to the virtuous members of the congregation—if
there were any whose consciences were completely clear—
and a good many sighs of relief must have been breathed
when this feature of the service was over.

Sometimes there was a lighter side to meeting. Perhaps
a young couple had been recently married—by the civil authorities since a religious ceremony was considered Popish
—and the young people were invited to step forward and
show their wedding finery. The bridegroom in his new
suit of homespun gray, his ears burning, would come from
his side of the church, falling over his new buckled shoes.
The bride, dressed now very much like the older women, in
gray, would appear from her side, blushing prettily and
perhaps wearing a scarlet cloak, since all Puritan clothes
were not drab. In the Dorothy Quincy house in Quincy,
Massachusetts, may be seen one of these cloaks, a bright
enough garment for Red Riding Hood.

The old meetinghouses were so cold that warm clothes
were a necessity for a large part of the year but even these
did not always mean comfort. We have in our attic a homemade foot warmer for use in church. It is an oblong box of

black cherry with a wrought-iron handle and a number of small openings. Inside is a piece of soapstone. When heated, this stays warm for a long time. We also have a comparatively sophisticated and modern apparatus consisting of a square tin box in a hardwood frame. The tin, which held hot coals, is perforated in a regular pattern.

We suppose that the great grandmother who owned the soapstone would shake her head and say, "This modern generation is brought up altogether too soft. I don't see any sense carrying a lot of hot coals around. What are we coming to?"

What they were coming to, probably with grandmother's intense disapproval, was stoves. We have heard about the stove feuds of so many churches that we assume the story must be true of at least one of them. Perhaps Litchfield, Connecticut, has the best claim to this bit of folklore. When the question of stoves came up there, the congregation immediately divided into a Stove and Anti-Stove party, but there were enough members opposed to chilblains and pneumonia for the motion for stoves to be carried.

Before many chilly Sundays had passed, the stoves were set up. They were, no doubt, masterpieces of ironwork with heads of cherubs, Chippendale legs, egg-and-dart molding, and other decorations more appropriate to marble temples under hot, blue skies. These stoves were equipped with long pipes, which wandered about ready to radiate warmth and comfort. On the first really frosty Sunday a large congregation assembled to test the stoves. The Stove party looked with pride at the polished ironwork and basked happily in the unaccustomed warmth. Some brave spirits even left their foot stoves behind. Others went so far as to remove their Paisley shawls. The anti-stove adherents went even farther. One lady is said to have fanned herself ostentatiously during most of the service, pausing only to wipe from her brow the perspiration brought on by the stifling heat.

When the service was over, someone happened to touch one of the stoves.

8. LITCHFIELD, CONNECTICUT. A memorable stove feud took place here.

It was cold, cold as an iron stove!

A section of pipe connecting stove and chimney was missing. It had been impossible to start the fire that morning.

Before this white church with its row of Ionic columns, stretches Litchfield Green, surely one of the most peacefully lovely in all New England. The fine white houses, the county courthouse, the graceful arches of the elms, the clipped turf make a stenciled pattern for a village green.

The town of Litchfield, settled about 1720, lies on a beautiful plateau east of the Housatonic Valley. Not far from the green, in what is probably the oldest house, Ethan Allen was born. He moved to Vermont when he was still young but his native state has cause to remember him. Allen's activities in keeping Vermont out of the hands of the Yorkers —as the inhabitants of New York state are still referred to in Vermont, and with a peculiar intonation—were of a sort to call attention to him and his Green Mountain Boys. He was branded as an outlaw with a price of one hundred and fifty pounds upon his head, but he had a faculty of being somewhere else when wanted and all his followers were loyal.

Connecticut authorized Allen to raise a regiment of rangers for an attack on Fort Ticonderoga. So many Connecticut men, more than two hundred, enlisted under Allen that he took command when they refused to serve under Benedict Arnold. Just what Allen said to the sleepy commander of Ticonderoga the night he demanded the surrender of the fort is good for an argument any time.

We were eating a fine piece of broiled Gaspé salmon in a Vermont hotel once when we heard a man at the next table say mildly and not very loud, "I have always understood that Ethan Allen demanded the surrender 'In the name of the Great Jehovah and of the Continental Congress.' "

Immediately three conscientious Vermonters left their tables and approched that of the speaker. One of them pounded on it, shouting, "What Allen said was 'In the name of the Continental Congress, by God!' Whereupon a very

9. WAYLAND, MASSACHUSETTS. In such a meetinghouse, mothers of big families were glad to let tithingmen take care of discipline.

small man with a very large voice maintained that Allen would never have mentioned either Jehovah or the Continental Congress.

"He made it a lot shorter than that," said the small man, and stumped back to his chicken pie.

We got the impression he had been at Fort Ticonderoga himself.

Anyone fond of eating dinner in peace is recommended not to bring up this topic in the dining room of the Montpelier Tavern.

Allen had ideas about transmigration of souls and planned to be reincarnated in a white horse. We never see one beside a red barn in a green pasture without wondering if from him we could get some light on that conversation at Ticonderoga.

It is safe to assume that Allen spent little time in the meetinghouse at Litchfield or, indeed, in any other. His skepticism so shocked his contemporaries that it is not hard to detect a certain note of satisfaction in the entry made by the president of Yale, Ezra Stiles, in his diary for the year 1789, "Feb. 13—Genl. Ethan Allen of Vermont died & went to hell this day."

Allen might not have had the patience to listen to lengthy sermons, but the congregation generally would have felt cheated if the discourse had been brief. Besides Sunday meeting was often the only time that neighbors saw each other, the only time many of them took from their long days of exhausting work. Perhaps the men had some recreation. They could hunt and fish with the reasonable excuse of supplying the family with food, but for the women going to meeting was often the only outing. It must have been restful to the mother of a big family to have a day when she did not cook anything but fed the family what she had prepared the day before. It must have been pleasant, too, after she had crammed the children into clean clothes and polished their faces, to sit quietly and let the tithingman take care of discipline. Those three-hour sermons probably often seemed to her all too short.

10. SOUTH SUTTON, NEW HAMPSHIRE. On Old Home Day this meetinghouse assumes a nineteenth-century air.

[51]

Through a large part of the nineteenth century going to meeting was still the social event of the week. People enjoyed it as much as the cheerful group we see driving away from the meetinghouse at South Sutton, New Hampshire. On Old Home Day, attics are ransacked for costumes of the last century, horses are hitched to ancient vehicles, and everyone goes to service in the meetinghouse.

We make two mistakes about the old days. One is to think of them as the good old days, to feel that if we had only been born earlier our troubles would never have occurred. The other is to see them as entirely grim and dreary. The truth lies somewhere between. There are hard days in all periods; pleasant days, too.

CHAPTER 3

The Tavern, a Recognized Need

Sometimes they called it an ordinary, sometimes an inn, a hostel, or a public house, but usually it was a tavern. Whatever it was called, it stood near the village common and frequently was next to the meetinghouse. This was no accident. On winter days the congregation needed a place to thaw out after the long sermon and there are records indicating that this need was recognized. In Boston in 1651, a man was granted "libertie to keep a house of Common entertainment if the Countie Court consent, provided he keep it near the new meetinghouse."

Before a permanent meetinghouse was built, the tavern was sometimes used for services. In Providence, Roger Williams preached in a tavern for years. At Little Compton, on the other hand, a meetinghouse became a tavern. The Great House at Charlestown, Massachusetts, where Governor Winthrop once lived, later became a meetinghouse and later still a tavern called The Three Cranes.

Court was often held in the taverns and was announced by the beating of drums. The drummers were paid two shillings a day. Taverns, in fact, were respectable places and their owners were dependable and sober men. The innkeeper in Duxbury in 1678 was allowed "to sell liquors unto such sober minded neighbors, as hee shall think meet, soe hee shall sell not less than the quantitie of a gallon att a time to one person, and not in smaller quantities by retaile to the occasion of drunkeness."

If we could enter one of the earliest of these houses of common entertainment, the first thing that would strike us would be its small size. We usually think of the old inns with spacious rooms and polished floors, a joint of meat roasting on a spit in a vast fireplace, great steaming punch bowls, enormous plum puddings, and candlelight with a jovial innkeeper carrying in the boar's head wreathed with bay and rosemary. Unfortunately this Christmas-card picture is far from accurate. The ordinaries of seventeenth-century New England were actually small, dark, grimly cold or stuffily hot according to the season, and poorly furnished. Since they were ill-lighted and since soap and water were both luxuries, they were undoubtedly dirty. The floors were often of earth, trodden hard, and perhaps, as a gesture toward cleanliness, covered with sand.

Not long before this time in even the grandest of English houses floors were covered with rushes. As these grew filthy— the dogs buried their bones among them—fresh rushes were thrown down on top of the old ones until the family was forced to move out and leave the house "to sweeten." They left to live in just as unsanitary a way in other tapestry-hung, rush-floored rooms, compared to which earthen floors strewn with fresh sand were models of cleanliness.

Innkeepers had their problems as this old notice shows:

> Rules of the tavern
> Fourpence a night for bed
> Sixpence with supper
>   No more than five to sleep in one bed
> No boots to be worn in bed
> Organ grinders to sleep in the wash house
> No Razor Grinders or Tinkers taken in.

Although today the distances between village greens seem short, as we drive from one to another, it was once a great undertaking to reach a lodging for the night. From Madam Sarah Knight's diary—she made the journey from Boston to New York in 1704—we get some idea of what it meant to travel between taverns. Madam Knight's business in New York was prosaic—the settlement of an estate—but she evidently regarded her journeys from one village tavern to the next as a series of adventures. From her diary we get an impression of the courage it took for a woman to travel alone at that time. A modern trip through the jungles of Central Africa could hardly be more uncomfortable than the eighteenth-century journey from Boston to New York.

Madam Knight came naturally by her intrepid and unconventional character. Her father was a traveler, too. Once he went on a journey that lasted three years. When he got home, one Sunday morning and met his wife on the doorstep of their house, he kissed her. Then he spent the next two hours in the stocks "for lewd and indecorous conduct."

His daughter's first difficulties began in Dedham where she had trouble securing a guide for the next twelve miles. Everyone in the tavern was enjoying the warmth of the fireside and a drink of cider or mulled ale, but finally a certain man, referred to as John, agreed to guide her. The diary notes that:

His shade on his Hors resembled a Globe on a gate post . . . Thus jogging on with an easy pace, my guide telling mee it was dangero's to Ride hard in the Night (wh. his horse had the sence to avoid) Hee entertained me with . . . the eminent Dangers he had escaped, so remembring . . . the Knight of the Oracle I didn't know but I had met a Prince disguis'd.

Eventually they came to the ordinary where Madam Knight was to lodge, and she writes:

But I had not gone many steps into the Room, ere I was interrogated by a young lady to this purpose (viz) Law for mee—what in the world brings you here at this time of a night? I never see a woman on the Rode so dreadful late in all the days of my versall life . . . And then run upstairs and putts on two or three Rings (or else I had not seen them before) and returning sett herself just before me, showing the way to Reding, that I might see her ornaments . . . she conducted me to a parlour in a little back lento wch was almst fill'd with the bedstead wch was so high I was forced to climb on a chair to gitt up to ye wretched bed that lay on it . . .

The other taverns Madam Knight visited were equally uncomfortable and the roads between them were rocky and muddy by turns. Streams had to be forded, although sometimes there was a ferry. Once her guide swam her horse over the river while she crossed in a canoe so unsteady that she wrote she did not dare to let a wry thought come into her mind or even think of Lot's wife for fear of finding herself in the water. It was two months before she was safely back in Boston again. In later years she herself became a tavern keeper. We hope she provided better food and hospitality than she encountered in her own travels. In any case her genial and humorous approach to life must certainly have been an asset.

Evidently there was no luxury in these early taverns, but at least the charges were reasonable. A tavern bill of the early eighteenth century indicates that dinner was ninepence, a bowl of toddy the same. A bill for Ordination Day, an occasion when ministers came together from many towns and enjoyed a special brew called ordination beer, reads:

	£	s	d
To Keeping Ministers		2	4
2 Mugs Tody		5	10
5 segars		3	
1 pint wine			9
3 Lodgings		9	
3 Bitters			9
3 Breakfasts		3	6
15 Boles Punch	1	0	0
24 Dinners	1	16	
11 Bottles wine		3	10
5 Mugs Flip		5	10
5 Boles punch		6	
3 Boles Tody		3	6

11. LEXINGTON, MASSACHUSETTS. From the Buckman Tavern the minutemen went out to line up on the green that morning
of the nineteenth of April.

A note on the bill reads, "All paid for except the Minister's Rum."

Later in the century, stagecoaches made travel somewhat more comfortable and less perilous than it was in Madam Knight's day. It is still easy to imagine these picturesque conveyances before such old taverns as the Wright Tavern or the Colonial Inn at Concord, the Publick House at Sturbridge, the Buckman Tavern at Lexington, the Wayside Inn at Sudbury, the Groton Inn at Groton—all in Massachusetts. In New England there are many other historic inns that are close to the village greens, among them the Hanover Inn and the Walpole Inn in New Hampshire; the Woodstock, Middlebury, and Manchester inns across the river in Vermont; and in Connecticut the Ben Grosvenor Inn at Pomfret and the Windham Inn at Windham, which was built in 1760 and, though remodeled, keeps much of its old appearance. These are taverns where the traveler today may still find hospitality.

The old taverns entertained not only ministers but soldiers as well. On training day on the village common there might be hundreds of visitors, the recruits and their families and neighbors who came to see them drill. During the long period of the French and Indian War, men drilled endlessly on the greens. Windham Green is, indeed, famous for an episode of that time when the threat of Indian attack was always in men's minds.

One summer night the people of Windham were disturbed by a strange sound. It came from the east, a weird throbbing like an Indian war whoop. It swelled and seemed to come nearer. The frightened villagers thought they could make out the names of two men, well known in the town and the country around. The voices seemed to demand the surrender of "Colonel Dyer and Elderkin too!"

Over and over the cry was repeated and ever louder. The villagers seized their guns and powder horns. They took their stands at windows and behind trees and waited for

12. WINDHAM, CONNECTICUT. This old inn built in 1760 for travelers in stagecoaches offers hospitality today.

the attack. All night the cries continued. Toward dawn they decreased and at last died completely away.

Still armed, the men of Windham set out to find the place from which the cries had come. They found it—a dry hollow, which had held a small pond until days of drought had dried it up. There they beheld the bodies of thousands of dead frogs. The Battle of the Frogs—as it is still called in Windham—was a battle which the frogs fought for the last drops of the muddy water. Eventually it was commemorated by a Windham bank which issued notes with pictures of the fighting frogs and portraits of Colonel Dyer and Elderkin too.

Many of these old New England inns were visited by George Washington during the early days of the Revolution and on his journey through New England when he was President of the United States. We are in the habit of thinking of Washington as a classically stern profile on a postage stamp or standing stiffly in a flowing cloak during the crossing of the Delaware or perhaps sitting in dignity before a crimson curtain. It is pleasant, for a change, to think of his human enjoyment of the hospitality of a tavern in Spencer, Massachusetts. "A pretty good house," he called it, and he said to the owner's wife, "Madam, your bread is beautiful!" On this same journey, he passed by the common at Worcester. "He was dressed in a brown suit and pleasure glowed on every countenance as he came along." He had a genial way of giving little girls his torn riding gloves to mend. Then when the glove was returned, he would reward the young seamstresses and kiss them on the cheek. One of them refused to have her face washed for a week afterwards!

He reached the tavern at Uxbridge, Massachusetts, one cold wet night after a long journey in the rain and was so delighted with his welcome that he later wrote to the proprietor:

Sir: being informed that you have given my name to one of your sons and called another after Mrs. Washington's family, and being moreover very much pleased with the modest and innocent looks of your two daughters Patty and Polly, I do for these reasons send each of these girls a piece of chintz and to Patty, who bears the name of Mrs. Washington and who waited on us more than Polly did, I send five guineas with which she may buy herself any little ornaments she wants or she may dispose of them in any other manner more agreeable to herself. As I do not give these things with a view to have it talked of or even known, the less said about it the better it will please me, but that I may be sure the chintz and money have got safe to hand, let Patty, who I dare say is equal to it, write me a line informing me thereof directed to the President of the United States at New York. I wish you and your family well and am your humble servant

George Washington.

Many of the old taverns, which flourished during the eighteenth century, dropped into insignificance with the coming of the railroads in the nineteenth, and then were miraculously revived in the twentieth by the demands of automobile traffic. One of the old inns which has seen the various changes of transportation since 1747 and is still showing hospitality to travellers is the Wright Tavern at Concord, Massachusetts.

Naturally in two centuries it has seen many changes. Although it was once the property of the First Parish Church, the white church with the gold-capped steeple that stands near it, it is actually older than the present church building. The land on which the tavern stands was once part of the training ground and the lot was deeded to its owner with the understanding that he must improve the training ground and "keep it from wasting away." Monument Square with its smoothly mown grass was formerly an unseeded piece of ground, dusty and muddy by turns under the feet of drilling soldiers. On training days their horses kicked and stamped at the rows of hitching posts there. The village bakery was in the cellar of the tavern and boys carrying loaded trays wriggled through the crowd, selling freshly browned cookies and buns, still warm from the oven, to the hungry soldiers. The taproom on the ground floor of the Wright Tavern took care of the thirsty.

13. CONCORD, MASSACHUSETTS. The British made the Wright Tavern their headquarters on the day of Concord Fight.

On the nineteenth of April, 1775, the taproom was full of scarlet coats, for Major Pitcairn and Colonel Smith made their headquarters there. One of them, probably Colonel Smith, though the speech has been attributed to Major Pitcairn, stirred his toddy with his finger, saying that before night he would stir the blood of the Yankee rebels as he did the toddy that morning.

James Wright, the landlord, who served this prophetic glass, kept the tavern for only a year, but his name clings to the old building. It is painted barn-red now, but has been at times white and yellow. Inside, the taproom retains much of its old appearance. Where the training-day buns were baked, typical New England food is still cooked in the basement, though with modern equipment. Upstairs there are interesting old pieces of furniture, old prints, and mementoes of what is locally known as Concord Fight.

There are two kinds of taverns on the New England greens. The first, of which the Wright Tavern is an example, was built for a tavern and has a long history as such. The second is an old dwelling which has become a house of common entertainment because at some period in its existence, often fairly recently, someone noticed that it was conveniently placed for such a purpose and remodeled it for public use. Visitors to Concord can visit a building of this second type simply by walking across Monument Square to the long, low, rambling gray structure that is the Colonial Inn.

The way in which this inn grew into its present form is typical of the casual development of such hostelries. It is composed of three old buildings with their original staircases, including one that ends abruptly against a ceiling. Somewhere in its walls the inn conceals timbers cut in the seventeenth century to build Concord's first meetinghouse. The oldest visible part is the house on the eastern end, at the right, as you face the inn. It stands on land once owned by the Rev. Peter Bulkeley, the first minister of the town.

14. CONCORD, MASSACHUSETTS. In the Colonial Inn behind the monument once lived Henry David Thoreau and Deacon White,
the exacting Sabbath-Day observer.

This house, probably built towards the close of the seventeenth century, was occupied by various members of the Minot family during the early part of the eighteenth century and later came into the possession of the Thoreau family. From its windows, young Henry David Thoreau used to watch the crows wheeling against the sky; from its door one of his aunts is said to have stolen out one night to pay the tax that Thoreau had refused a government that supported slavery.

The central portion of the inn was once a one-story building in which Deacon White kept store. He added the second story and lived above the store for a time. Then he built the western end of the inn for a dwelling and his partner, whose name was Shattuck, lived above the store.

Deacon White was one of those "characters" dear to New England hearts. He was a teetotaller, but he sold spirits, taking care to have them, his customers alleged "so weak that they wouldn't run down hill." The gun powder he sold was no more powerful than the rum. A whole keg of it once caught fire and burned peacefully without exploding. The Deacon was kind to children, giving them sweets and books and letting them listen to his wonderful parrot, who could imitate every bird in Concord, but the Deacon became a stern and implacable figure on Sundays. He had the task of preventing traffic on the Lowell Road. Anyone who broke the Sabbath by trying to drive past the Deacon's place was disciplined.

Once a teamster was stopped on Sunday morning and told that he could go no further until evening. This particular offender decided to be as troublesome as possible. He hitched his horses, followed the Whites to church, and sat in the pew with them, his dusty white smock in strange contrast to the Deacon's black broadcloth and Mrs. White's equally dignified black silk. After church he followed them home and sat down at the dinner table with them, eating heartily. His appetite was still good at tea time and also at supper. After supper the Deacon stood with his watch in his hand and when it informed him that the Sabbath was over said, "You may go now, Sir."

Whenever the teamster told the story of this Sabbath-day entertainment, he always added, "I guess the Deacon got the worst of it."

The Deacon's store sold a little of everything—"West India goods," boots, tea, pantaloons, raisins. No doubt there was a cracker barrel, too. Certainly it is pleasant to find one still in the country store around the corner from the inn. Some of the contents of the new store would no doubt surprise the Deacon, but there is a friendly atmosphere about it which would make him feel at home. It would surprise him too to find that his house and his store and the Thoreaus' house were now welcoming travelers along the Lowell Road, even on Sundays, though not detaining them forcibly.

Like many other old New England houses now used as taverns, the Colonial Inn contains interesting furniture, some of it very nearly as old as the house itself. There are sofas, an old pine settle, guns, powder horns, and mirrors that have reflected through the years the events which the three houses have witnessed. Most interesting in the collection is a framed set of forty blue and white tiles representing the fight at the bridge.

The bridge appears as a distinctly precarious structure. At one end of it the front rank of the British is firing a volley, but the rear ranks are retreating as fast as the short legs of the men will let them. There is an extraordinary amount of smoke—perhaps some of Deacon White's powder is burning—and through it the Americans are running downhill towards the bridge. Sometimes there are legs without heads trotting through the smoke and sometimes heads without legs seem to be blown along above it.

For a more realistic version of the battle, we like the splendidly executed scale model at the Concord Antiquarian Society. The society also has one of the most complete and beautifully arranged collections of New England furniture

[66]

to be found in any museum. If we wished to get an idea of the houses from the seventeenth century on into the nineteenth and could visit only one collection, this would be our choice.

For those who have plenty of time, there are several Concord houses, interesting for historical and literary associations, which are open to the public. A favorite with most visitors is Orchard House, where *Little Women* was written. The Alcotts were living there when a friend of our grandmother's went out to Concord to see them. Mrs. Alcott was busy in the kitchen, but Mr. Alcott was at leisure and greeted the visitor with his usual sweet, vague friendliness and sat down with him on the doorstep in the sunshine. Bronson Alcott smiled kindly at his wife as she passed them on her way to the woodpile and continued to bend an approving glance upon her as she came back with her apron full of small sticks and stooped to pick up some chips she had dropped.

Then he turned the same kindly smile upon the visitor and observed, "How beautiful is labor!"

The visitor carried in the next load of wood.

The feeling that you might look out through the windows of the Colonial Inn or the Wright Tavern and see Alcott or Emerson, Thoreau or Hawthorne walking across the square is part of the charm of both these old buildings. Concord never seems to lose touch with its past. The links are so many and so varied—Emerson's study, the monuments on the green (they call an honor roll a glory board in Concord), old houses with uneven floors where you step up into one room and down into the next, a bullet hole carefully protected by glass, the tall, white-fluted pillars of the church, the tavern, the inn, the hill near the green and the graves on it—each is part of the chain of memory.

Better than flip glasses or clusters of purple Concord grapes, ivy-covered boulders and elm-vaulted roads, two gravestones help us to step back into Concord's past. These bear inscriptions which clearly indicate what qualities the people of this quiet country town admired in their fellow citizens. The first is on the gravestone of Colonel James Barrett, who fought against the British on the nineteenth of April in 1775. The inscription is one of many that have dignity and beauty and the stone, high up on the hillside, is one of the handsomest we have even seen in an old graveyard.

It is a large slab of slate. At the top, instead of the more usual skull-like cherub's head, is frankly a skull and the words *Memento Mori* with crossed swords below. Skull and swords are in relief; so is the Barrett coat of arms and the border of oak leaves, a climbing vine, and flowers. Cut into the stone are these words:

<blockquote>
Here rests
in hope ye body of
Col. James Barrett
who departed this life
April 11, 1779 in the 69th year of his age.
Sudden the summons came and quick the flight
We trust to be with Christ in realms of light
In public & privit life he was courteous, benevolent & charitable, His fidelity, uprightness and
ability in various offices and employments justly
procured him esteem. For many years he represented this Town in General Court. He early stept
forward in ye contest with Britain & distinguished
himself in ye cause of America. His warm attach-
ment to & careful practice of ye religion of Christ
compleated his worthy character & with his other
virtues will preserve his memory and rank
it with that of the just, which is blessed
Oh reader, from this pale monument learn
Wisdom for Eternity; wisdom for
Thyself: and be reminded of thy fate
Which hastens on the swift wings of time
Death steals upon you like a midnight thief
His step is secret but yet sure and may
Be near and unexpected
</blockquote>

Colonel Barrett was one of the great men of his time and place. To one of the humblest of her citizens, Concord paid tribute on another stone. This is of slate, too, but has no ornament, except a simple linear border easily made in the soft stone.

> God wills us free, man wills us slaves
> I will as God wills: God's will be done.
> > Here lies the body of
> > > John Jack
> > a native of Africa who died
> > March 1773 aged about 68 years.
> > Tho' born in a land of slavery,
> > He was born free.
> > Tho' he lived in a land of liberty,
> > He lived a slave.
> > Till by his honest, tho' stolen labors,
> > He acquired the source of slavery,
> > Which gave him his freedom;
> > Tho' not long before
> > Death the grand tyrant
> > Gave him his final emancipation
> > And set him on a footing with wings
> > Tho' a slave to vice
> > He practised those virtues
> > Without which kings are but slaves.

The people who engraved these words on stone lived in a town where the democracy they fought for was not only won, but used.

In that first battle for independence, two taverns played an important part. As we have mentioned, the Wright Tavern at Concord was the headquarters of the British. Earlier on the nineteenth the Americans had gathered in the Buckman Tavern at Lexington, a fine square white house and now open as a museum. Later in the day two wounded British soldiers were brought there and there one of them died.

Because of the use of the commons as training grounds,

the near-by taverns were a natural meeting place for soldiers and the obvious place for them to be carried when wounded. These eighteenth-century taverns were not, however, very different from the dwellings near them. Often the only public room was the kitchen, which differed from other country kitchens only in having a cupboard for bottles and glasses in one corner with a bar across it. The big fireplace with its assortment of hardware—toasters, long-handled shovels called peels with which bread was taken out of Dutch ovens, equally long-handled skillets in which the cook could fry salt pork without scorching her face, a tin kitchen for roasting meat, three-legged kettles of various sizes—was a necessity. Near the fireplace there was usually a high-backed settle. With that, a few benches, and some rush-bottomed chairs, a flip iron for scorching a pungent mixture of beer, maple syrup, pumpkin, and rum, a landlord was ready for business.

He was fortunate if his house stood on the village green, but there were many taverns in other places. Inns sprang up where two roads crossed each other or separated, or at a convenient distance from some large town where the stage had to change horses, or perhaps simply anywhere a man had a wife energetic enough to add tavern-keeping to her other occupations. One unlucky innkeeper lost his wife and soon after his license, on the ground that he was not "so well fitted as before to keep an inn."

Whether it stood on the green or by itself at the top of a steep hill—a good situation because visitors did not like to go down without taking some refreshment and were so out of breath when they came up that they had to stop—life gravitated to the old taverns. Dancing bears, scissor-grinders, tin peddlers, sailors home from the sea, fiddlers ready to play for contra dances, soldiers pitching pennies on the barroom floor, cobblers, candlemakers, wandering portrait painters, all passed along the roads and stopped at the taverns. And of course, there were the regular customers, as much a part of the furniture as the flip glasses, the swizzle sticks, and the pewter mugs. One of these faithful patrons swallowed what seemed to be his last drink in a Vermont tavern. His friends picked him up, put him on a door, and carried him solemnly across the common to break the news to his widow. When she answered their knock, they had not found words to tell her what had happened but a voice from the stretcher saved them the trouble.

"Mehitabel," it said, "ain't you got the rum ready to treat the bearers?"

On many greens through New England, it is still possible to stay in an old tavern—or at least to have a meal there—and to find them today, it is not necessary to travel as Madam Knight did. It is not, however, possible to find them at sixty miles an hour. A little time is needed, a little of the leisure that belonged to that era when a good day's journey was twenty miles and when at the end of it you were ready for dinner. When the waiter rang the bell, you sat down to a repast of venison, wild turkey, oysters, bear meat, lobster, partridge, hasty pudding, and three kinds of pie. And it was all yours for just two shillings!

15. WRENTHAM, MASSACHUSETTS. Many houses like this one of white clapboards face on village greens.

CHAPTER *4*

Houses Provide the Frame

No picture is complete without a frame. We pause at many a village green because of what surrounds it, rather than for the green itself. True there are certain deserted villages in New England—Dogtown near Gloucester in Massachusetts, Jerusalem in Vermont—where we find a certain wistful charm in the cellar holes of long-vanished houses, in grass-grown roads, in forgotten gravestones among the goldenrod, but it is the houses still standing to which we look to reveal to us something of the past.

To describe, or even to enumerate, all the interesting old houses that face the commons of New England towns would be a fascinating task, but one that would fill the kind of volume which small children are given to sit on when a Chippendale chair leaves them with only their eyes above the edge of the table. The word, old, covers so wide a range. It may be used to describe weathered gabled buildings of the seventeenth century or tall brick mansions of the early nineteenth. Even the mansard-roofed houses of the sixties now belong to a vanished past and little Gothic cottages with pointed windows and scrollwork along the eaves have become "quaint," instead of merely inconvenient and out of style. If we only include houses built before the jig saw and during the period when ready-made millwork was still as unknown as ready-made waistcoats, we still find an enormous number of old houses in a great many styles. There are rambling, weather-beaten farmhouses with sheds and barns and lean-tos, compact salt-box houses with big central chimneys, square white houses of wood from which men rode to the Battle of Lexington, mansions with classic porches, and story-and-a-half cottages. Cape Cod has given its name to these last. Actually they are all through New England and usually of wood, though sometimes of brick, and occasionally of stone, but providing in any case the kind of shelter that architects claim women always demand—a small house with a great many large rooms.

Wood, usually painted white, was the favorite material for the houses on the green because wood was readily available, but bricks were necessary for chimneys and in most villages a brickyard was an early project. There is the same difference between handmade brick and the modern factory-made product as there is between homemade bread and the plaster of Paris loaves efficiently turned out by the thousand. Just as bread baked at home may come out of the oven any shade from ivory to golden brown—in moments of absent-mindedness it may even emerge the color and consistency of an overshoe—so old bricks varied from one baking to another from soft rose-pink to a dark plum that is almost black. Like bread, too, the old bricks had pleasing irregularities of texture. Some builders preferred them to wood for walls as well as chimneys, sometimes just for the ends of the house, but on occasion also for the main structure. Even so, porches and cornices and outbuildings were usually built of wood.

Different types of roofs—gables, gambrels, hip roofs—make different profiles against the sky. Doorways range from the sturdy simplicity of the seventeenth-century entrances to the sophisticated elegance of pillared porches, interpreting classic Greek in carved pine. These doorways and the fanlights above them are a study in themselves and so are the porches that shelter them. Light entered the old house through bull's-eyes of handblown glass, through diamond-sectioned casements, through the thin panes of twelve-over-twelves, through the purple glass of the houses on Boston Common, or the Palladian windows that look on Salem's Washington Square.

In this Square and along the streets near by, the visitor can easily follow the development of the New England house as it emerged from the almost medieval irregularity of dwellings like the House of the Seven Gables to the classic stateliness of the Chestnut Street mansions of the Federal period. From these different houses—many of them open to the public—it is possible to know life in Salem from the days of its earliest settlement to the time when so many ships sailed to the Orient that, in China, Salem was thought of as a separate country of immense wealth and inhabited by a race of men different from all others. Indeed, as we think of the young men of Salem who in their early twenties became captains of ships and retired from the sea with immense fortunes by the time they were thirty, they do seem a race apart.

Henry Hudson Kitson's statue of Roger Conant, founder of Salem, presides over Washington Square and recalls the days before the town built tall brick chimneys joined in pairs, balustrades around imposing hip roofs, lofty Corinthian columns before entrances, and intricately carved cornices to support porches. The first buildings of the town were not on a green but near the sea. Today in Pioneer Village in Forest River Park you may see reproductions of the dugouts, the dark little cabins, the pits for sawing wood, the stocks and the whipping post, and even the herbs that grew in Puritan gardens in the early days. Governor Endicott's "fayre house" has been rebuilt there with its generous fireplace and great central chimney. It is the largest house in the settlement but seems oddly cramped for a governor's mansion. The primitive discomfort of this early village is an interesting contrast to the houses of Salem's sailing days.

16. SALEM, MASSACHUSETTS. These handsome houses look upon Washington Square, one of the most extensive of all village greens.

We still feel this contrast as we visit the House of the Seven Gables. There were many old gabled houses still standing in Salem when Hawthorne wrote the story this house recalls. He always insisted he had no special house in mind, but the house that bears the title fits his description well enough, and it is easy to accept uncritically the guide's definite assertions about the shop and the secret staircase and "Clifford's room." As we rested in the lovely quiet garden and looked up at the weathered gables against the sky, we remembered that in 1668, when the house was built, London was just recovering from the Great Fire in which many buildings just like this one with overhanging second stories and wooden, acorn-shaped pendrils and small-paned windows were destroyed.

Hawthorne himself was born in a house of an only slightly later type, a gambrel-roofed structure, still standing on Union Street not far from Washington Square. The old Custom House where he worked is close at hand, too, and near it is the oldest brick house in Salem, the Richard Derby House. This was built in 1762 and has many resemblances to later mansions—dentiled cornices, paired chimneys at the ends, a doorway with a pediment—but its gambrel roof links it with an earlier period. Such roofs were better suited to the climate of New England with its deep winter snow than were roofs of many gables where snow collected between and, in melting, too often found its way through shingles and into rooms below.

The gambrel-roofed houses with their roomy third stories were evolving into an architectural style at once practical and beautiful—the square, hip-roofed house which Samuel McIntire so magnificently designed. On Washington Square, and near by on Essex and Chestnut Streets, may be seen the work of this genius who turned from ships to dwellings and even to the designing of furniture for spacious parlors and dining rooms. Like the builders of the meetinghouses, he showed great skill in translating ideas originally intended for brick and stone into wood, as in the Peirce-Nichols

House on Federal Street. There, even the gatepost urns are carved from solid blocks of wood to harmonize with the Doric pediment above the door and the classic elegance of the fluted pilasters. The inside woodwork is also executed with marvelous delicacy, the smallest ornaments on chimney piece and doorway contributing to the whole handsome effect. The Pingree House on Essex Street, like the houses facing the Square, belongs to the period when McIntire built in brick. Among the finest are the Boardman House at Number 82, the Waters House at Number 80, and the Lyman House at Number 90. No two are alike, yet they harmonize beautifully and lend to the eight acres of Washington Square a distinction that is found on no other common in New England.

Not all McIntire's houses, however, are large and impressive. On the streets leading away from the common are more modest structures suggesting the compactness of a ship. In the Kimball House, for instance, just off the Square, McIntire builds a small entrance hall and pulls up through it a circular staircase as graceful as a new shaving just uncurled, and carves—it is said with his own hands—the eagle and flag-draped shield and the perfectly executed balls and ropes of the chimney piece. Half a century ago (about the time we ate our first Salem Gibraltar) two ladies, almost a hundred years old, were living in the Kimball House. It was said they attributed their great age and perfect health to shutting the house up tightly about November first, never going out of it, keeping it at eighty degrees throughout the winter, and eating mince pie every day—this, of course, from blue Canton china since the husband of one of them had been a sea captain.

In some way all these Salem houses are reminiscent of trade with the Orient, but Salem ships also voyaged to the West Indies, to Leghorn, and Malaga, and to the coast of Africa, where they traded with dark-skinned native potentates for ivory, gold dust, and camphor wood. In those glorious days a Salem boy who lived on the common could be on the wharves in a few minutes and see forests of masts, men unloading hogsheads of molasses and barrels of sugar, or bringing aboard casks of New England rum. He could watch the spinning of ropes in the rope walks or the great sails for a clipper ship being sewn in a sail loft. He might press his nose against windows where he could see, along with the familiar gingerbread and candy, bolts of crimson cloth for breeches, piles of bandanas and handkerchiefs that had come from Barcelona, and great mounds of lemons from Italy. He could easily imagine himself a fine captain with silver buttons on his coat, a hat cocked jauntily over one eye, a spyglass under his arm, and as many Salem Gibraltars—that most delicious of all white sugar candies— as he could possibly eat.

Sailors, he knew, were different from other men. For one thing they wore different clothes, and you could always spot them by their bell-bottomed trousers, their thick pea jackets, checked shirts, shiny black hats, and by their bold expressions. When the famous Black Friday, May 19, 1780, occurred and Salem Common, as well as all of New England, was mysteriously darkened, "People in the streets grew melancholy and fear seized all except sailors; they went hallooing and frolicking through the streets and were reproved in vain; they cried to the ladies as they passed, 'Now you may take off your rolls and high caps and be d - - d.' "

These ladies, to whom William Pynchon refers in his diary, had probably patronized William Lang, a barber, who advertised about this time that "Ladies shall be attended to in the polite construction of rolls such as may tend to raise their heads to any pitch they desire."

At a time when even false hair had to be "politely" constructed, small boys could hardly have been blamed for envying sailors whose rough manners were reproved in vain. No wonder youngsters went to sea as early as they could. However, life ashore also had its excitements. Any boy who lived near the common saw minutemen drilling and watched them assemble when the news came that British troops under Colonel Leslie were marching toward Salem from Marblehead to seize the colonists' military equipment.

That day a great crowd of citizens, doubtless including every boy in town, gathered at the bridge which the British troops had to cross to reach Salem. The draw was raised and, had it not been for the moderation of Colonel Leslie, the War of the Revolution might have begun at this bridge and the shot heard round the world been fired in Salem, not Concord, and Washington Square instead of Lexington Common might now be known as the Battle Green. But Leslie explained if they would lower the draw and let him march his troops across, he would at once withdraw without damaging the town. The Americans agreed. Leslie marched his men some fifty yards beyond the bridge, then wheeled around, and his orders fulfilled, marched back toward Marblehead whence he had come.

As the British turned, a woman leaned from a window and called: "Go home and tell your master he sent you on a fool's errand. Do you think we were born in the woods to be frightened by owls?"

As a soldier pointed his musket at her, she screamed, "Fire if you have the courage. I doubt it."

This earlier, New England Barbara Frietchie had the satisfaction of the last word, for the soldier lowered his gun. Colonel Leslie was congratulated for his good sense by a man who had been busy arousing the countryside: "You have done right to march off," the messenger said, "for in a short time we shall have more men here than your soldiers have lice in their heads."

Beyond the commons of Salem and Boston with their gracious dwellings, in remote villages where neither of them ever set foot, the influence of Samuel McIntire and Charles Bulfinch, the two best-known New England architects of their time, can be seen throughout the countryside. Sometimes the name of one of them is connected with a brick mansion near one of these distant village greens, but neither could possibly have built all the houses attributed to him. It would of course be interesting to be able to say definitely that McIntire built a certain house, yet in a way it is more interesting to say that he did not; that in spite of the fact that his pencil never traced a line of its plan, there stands a house epitomizing the spirit of his work.

At Orford, New Hampshire, the beautiful General Wheeler House—still owned by the Wheeler family—is attributed to Bulfinch. Certainly it is fine enough to be his work. Not long before it was built, the Connecticut River north of Hanover ran through almost undiscovered country and the first settlers of Orford in 1761 traveled there over a footpath among huge trees. One young bride and bridegroom received their land as a wedding present. It had been purchased for a dollar an acre.

Half a century later the wilderness had been conquered and Orford already had begun to look as it does today. Ages before the white men came to America, the Connecticut River changed its course and cut a new channel for itself. On the old river bottom now grow the grass and trees of Orford's beautiful mall, above which rises a steep natural terrace made when the river left its old bank and flowed along a new course. On this terrace—locally called the Ridge—and across the mall from it grew up what Washington Irving called the most beautiful village he had ever seen.

"It is a charming place," he wrote. "Nature has done her utmost here."

True, nature has done much for Orford but the builders of the town also did their share. They laid out the broad street and the green mall leading to the common with its double row of maples and elms. They built along it one of the finest groups of houses of the Federal period to be found anywhere in America.

There are seven of them, all gleaming against the rich green of grass and trees, all alike in spirit but varied in design. It is the house at the southern end that is attributed to

Bulfinch. Architects run their hands over the moldings, note the carved balls on the pillars of the mantelpieces and the graceful curve at the top of the stair rail where most builders set a newel post, and feel little doubt that Bulfinch designed them. The other houses were built by talented local craftsmen in the same style as the Wheeler House. Whoever planned them achieved an air of elegance and distinction rare in any house but rarer still in a whole group. The Wheeler House is notable not only for its handsome façade, the arches over the windows, and the wrought iron above the porch, but for the mass of the long ell and outbuildings running back towards the hill behind the Ridge.

At the other end of the row, the four black-topped chimneys of the Howard-Dana House send their smoke up above the elms. This house was originally of red brick trimmed with white but has now been painted all white. It has a well-proportioned porch with columns and, like the Wheeler House, gives an impression of comfortable roominess. We accept this as characteristic of the whole group until we notice that one delightful little house is only a single story high. It has a hip roof, arched doorway, a fanlight, and a cornice as dignified and impressive as those of its larger neighbors, but all has been so carefully designed to harmonize with the small scale that it has the charm of a doll's house with everything perfectly carried out in miniature.

The effect of this avenue of shining houses is serene and restful. Many old houses, though beautiful in themselves, have been so elbowed and crowded by young upstarts that they lose their distinction. The houses that look out on the ridge at Orford have all the space they need: their own smooth lawns and the shady mall below. Before them flows the elm-bordered river sweeping in silvery curves through fertile meadows. Beyond the river, bare rocky cliffs, changing with the light from brown to amethyst and opal, tower in steep palisades. Behind the houses rise wooded hills and higher still Mount Cube's dark bulk touches the clouds.

When we walk along the mall and gaze up at the houses

17. Orford, New Hampshire. The Howard-Dana House on the Ridge is one of an elegant and distinguished group.

on the Ridge, we find it easy to slip back to the days when the placid water of the Connecticut was first churned up by Samuel Morey's steamboat. It is just as well in Orford not to suggest that Robert Fulton invented the steamboat. Morey had his boat running in 1793 long before Fulton's craft amazed people along the Hudson. Morey is said to have been so embittered by his failure to receive credit for his invention that he had his steamboat transported up to Lake Morey behind the palisades across the river and sank it.

There is always something a little ghostly and mysterious about the thought of a sunken ship, whether it is a Spanish galleon, a Yankee clipper, or even this almost forgotten steamboat. Oddly enough, the most vivid reminder of Morey's steamboat is also hidden. When one of the houses on the mall was being repapered a few years ago, a mural was discovered beneath the old paper showing eighteenth-century Orford with the steamboat puffing up the river. The mural has again been covered with paper but like the sunken boat itself, although it has vanished, it still remains.

The pattern of the square, hip-roofed house is often repeated around New England commons. One especially attractive example is the Bullock House at Royalston, Massachusetts, a sleepy hilltop village where the green is nearly half a mile long, where even the general store has a fan-lighted doorway, where white painted houses, large and small, shine as freshly among the maples as does the white marble of the war memorial.

The road runs through the middle of the common with wide greens on either side. Four roads leave the common, one at each corner, as they have since 1765 when the common was first laid out and they were only blazed trails through the deep woods. There is a story that on one of these trails an early settler once thought he heard lumbering toward him a cow that had strayed from the common. He went to drive it back and found himself facing an enormous moose. In spite of his surprise, he shot it and always regarded the meeting as a fortunate one: out of the hide he had a pair of leather

18. ROYALSTON, MASSACHUSETTS. A square white house with a beautiful
fence looks out on a sleepy hilltop common.

breeches made for himself, and for his bride, the saddle on which he brought her home to Royalston.

The town was named for Isaac Royal of Medford, the holder of one of the early grants of land on which the town was built and a contributor to the first meetinghouse. Royal was a Tory and during the Revolution it was suggested that the town should change its name, but the citizens saw no reason for belated ingratitude and it remains Royalston. It was the last town in Massachusetts to be disposed of by grants and charters. One of the grants was made for the curious reason that some of the settlers had buried there the bleached bones of British soldiers killed long before by the Indians while western Massachusetts was still wild country.

Good sense and brevity as well seem to have characterized Royalston town meetings. In 1778 a meeting was called "to hear the resolves of Congress and act thereon as the town may think proper." The report of the meeting records tersely: "Read the resolves of Congress. Voted to accept and abide by them."

It seems probable that this was done.

The inscription on the War Memorial—a flagpole set on a block of white marble—has some of this same directness:

TO REMIND US OF
JOHN ANTONIO FLAMATTI
WHO GAVE HIS LIFE
AND OF THOSE OTHER
SONS OF ROYALSTON
WHO WORE THEIR
COUNTRY'S UNIFORM
IN WORLD WAR TWO.

The names of other sons of the town are cut on two sides of the block and on the fourth is that of Calvin Bullock, whose family gave the memorial. There was white clematis in bloom on the white fence of the Bullock House, which is across the green from the flagpole, when we saw it. The clematis seemed essential to the design, adding as does the railing around the roof, a delicate airiness, an embroidered laciness to the square block of the house. Another of these graceful railings, different in design but with the same look of having been carved out of something no heavier than fresh snow, edges the roof of a house on the other side of the common. The secret of building well lasted long in this placid hill village. Even the mansard-roofed Town Hall did not whole heartedly accept the ugliness of its period but shows by its doorway and quoined corners that it remembers an earlier time.

We thought we had long ago lost the capacity to wonder over the links between quiet New England commons and the world outside, but we could not help a moment of surprise when we were told that an ex-empress, the former Empress Zita of Austria, is one of Royalston's summer visitors. Imperial splendors, even when they have vanished, seem incongruous with the precise neatness of a square white New England house, despite clematis on the fence. It reminds us of the contrasts in which Henry James delighted: American simplicity set off against sophisticated magnificence. We think of *The Wings of the Dove* and Milly Theale, dying in her great Venetian palace, or the Ververs in *The Golden Bowl* and their difficulties with the Italian prince. Joseph Hergesheimer used the same kind of theme in *Java Head* when a Salem sea captain brings home an oriental princess as his bride.

A contrast, stranger than those of fiction, almost became fact in Wiscasset, Maine. If all had gone well, Marie Antoinette might once have walked Wiscasset Common. Her name is still given to the house across the river where the best bedroom was made ready to receive her during the days of the Terror. Wiscasset was one of the busiest harbors in New England then and ships sailed up the Sheepscot River from many foreign ports. One of these Wiscasset vessels was the brig *Sally,* owned by Captain Clough, who also owned a square plain New England house, built in the ordinary way around a large central chimney. It was a comfortable house for its time and place but bleak and austere compared with the tapestry-hung magnificence of Versailles or even the artificial simplicity of the Petit Trianon.

Captain Clough was in a French port in 1793 and saw the outbreak of the blazing violence of the French Revolution. He was there when the streets of Paris were running with blood. One day his wife received a letter directing her to prepare to receive Marie Antoinette as her guest. Captain Clough's ship was in the Seine. The plan was complete and made with men who could be trusted.

"Well you know," he wrote, "that my sympathy has always been with her, even though I am an American born citizen and in America we trust no king but God. Prepare you the house not for a royal guest but a broken hearted woman."

It would not have been human nature if Captain Clough's family had not bustled about trying to make the house fit for a queen, even if she were a brokenhearted one, and we can imagine the scrubbing and polishing that went on and how the tasks were often and anxiously repeated as the months dragged on without news of the *Sally*. When at last she sailed up the river she contained splendid things—gowns of brocade with ruffles of lace, hangings of velvet and silk, a carved chest, gorgeous tapestries, rolls of wallpaper, vases of Sèvres porcelain—but there was no queen. The *Sally* had waited at Le Havre. The arrangements for smuggling Marie Antoinette out of prison seemed certain of success. A note was sent to her in a bouquet telling her that freedom was at hand.

But the jailer found the note. The next day the queen went to the guillotine.

She never saw Wiscasset's gently sloping common, perhaps the most beautiful in Maine, nor the many interesting buildings around it. Court is still held in the Lincoln County Court House where once was heard Daniel Webster's voice. Near the courthouse is the meetinghouse, a simple dignified structure with Ionic pillars along its porch. Mansions, built at the time when Wiscasset was almost as busy a port as Boston, face the common and show Palladian windows, pilasters, and elaborately carved cornices.

19. WISCASSET, MAINE. Sea captains built their houses on the most beautiful common in Maine.

20. WISCASSET, MAINE. The meetinghouse with stately Ionic columns presides over the peaceful slope of the common.

An idea of what the Queen of France might have found in a Wiscasset house, if her own brocades and porcelain had been left behind, may be obtained from Samuel Denny's will, which was recorded in the courthouse in 1771.

Itum I give unto my loving wife Catherine Denny . . . the best bed underbed and bedstead together with an Equal share of all that belong to beds both lining and wooling with the rest of my fether beds . . . the looking glass with black frame tabel and smorl trunk . . . the chist of drawers the best tea table . . . 6 tea cups and sarsers teakittel shugar dish crempot . . . with the best tongs shovel and belows three large and smorl silver spoons 6 puter plates and three puter dishes six best Earthurn plat fower best candlesticks the belmettel and brass scillit a pair of Iron dogs 2 flat Irons the box iron and 2 heters. Warming pan toster the great bibel 2 brass chafeendishes one large and one smorl spinning wheale 2 puter baisins 3 puter prongers . . . 3 wine glarsses 2 bekers 2 bowls . . . the silver can 6 common puter plats . . . together with a sute of curtains.

Where are these "itums" now? Doubtless some of them are in museums, and some of them, we hope, are treasured in Wiscasset houses. Some must have traveled far from the common and there must also be a few poor wanderers that pass from one Maine auction to another—the "common puter plats" and the "smorl spinning wheale" perhaps—and never find rest.

Typical of the smaller houses near most village greens is a story-and-a-half house known for obvious, and in spring, fragrant reasons, as Lilac Cottage. These compact houses, with roofs off which the snow slides easily, are well suited to the winter climate of the country. In time of blizzards, icicles, and chilblains, when you can see your breath in the halls of the big square mansions, houses like Lilac Cottage or those that face the green at West Newbury, Massachusetts, have the best of it.

Lord Timothy Dexter used often to pass by West Newbury Green in his big coach drawn by cream-colored horses, for this self-patented nobleman lived near by. Dexter was born in no such splendor as that of his Newburyport house

21. WEST NEWBURY, MASSACHUSETTS. Comfortable, compact New England houses face the frozen green.

and, during the early part of his life would doubtless have felt quite at home in any comfortable New England cottage. However, he was socially ambitious and having made a fortune, he moved to Newburyport, bought a fine mansion, decorated it according to his own ideas of magnificence and tried to push himself into society there—without success, as you will still be told if you are tactless enough to bring up the subject.

The basis of his fortune was partly a tannery, partly the sale of a cargo of warming pans in the West Indies. In his autobiography Dexter tells that, having dreamed for three nights that warming pans were needed in those tropical isles, he collected "no more than 42,000" and loaded them on nine vessels bound for the West Indies. There the pans were immediately sold, but not for warming beds with hot coals, but as ladles for use in sugar refineries!

Dexter's lucky speculation was immortalized in the coat of arms which he had painted on the panels of his coach—a dexter arm waving a warming pan with the motto: "By this I got ye."

Some of his ideas on architecture were as original as this on heraldry. He added a cupola to his house, also minarets, and an enormous eagle, gilded and with open wings. He employed a ship's carver to make statues of celebrated men and had them mounted on columns around his garden. These were painted appropriately with blue coats, buff waistcoats, brass buttons. Over the arched entrance was Washington with Adams on his right and Jefferson on his left. The three presidents survived Dexter, but their owner had some of the statues repainted to represent new characters from time to time.

One American general was made over into Napoleon. Dexter admired the Corsican and used to touch his great cocked hat to him as he passed the statue. Lord Timothy's own statue, cocked hat and all, was among the celebrities. He was represented holding a scroll with a brief statement of his achievements: "I am the first in the East; first in the West, and the greatest Philosopher in the known world."

Dexter appointed his own poet laureate, an ex-fish peddler, and had him dressed in black broadcloth with silver stars, silver-buckled shoes, and cocked hat. Thus turned out, the poet greeted his patron in a fifteen stanza poem which mentioned that

> *Lord Dexter like King Solomon*
> *Has gold and silver by the ton.*

Dexter himself worked in prose and produced his *Pickle for the Knowing Ones*. Even the knowingest ones have never been quite sure whether they could safely laugh at Dexter's ignorance or whether he was just possibly laughing at them. He did not punctuate his first edition but made up for it in the second by inserting—along with a page of punctuation marks—the following note:

"Mister Printer the nowing ones complane of my book the first edition had no stops I put in A nuf here and they may peper and salt it as they please."

Lord Dexter was not sufficiently satisfied with his lifetime position as the chief figure of both hemispheres but wished to be sure that it would be maintained properly after his death. He wanted to be present at his own funeral, so he sent out invitations to it, ordered mourning for his family, even found a minister to officiate. The procession marched solemnly through the shadows of the statues to the vault in the garden while Dexter watched from an upper window. Perhaps none of us would be satisfied with his own funeral. Before the visitors had left, Dexter began beating his wife for not crying hard enough over his coffin. He rests now in the Old Hill Burying Ground near Bartlett Mall, which is one of Newburyport's delightful expanses of green. The old county jail, where British prisoners were housed during the Revolution, is at the end of the mall. In another open green space, not central like a true village green, is Brown's Park with a statue of William Lloyd Garrison.

The old houses around the greens seem unchanging, but they are not really so. They smell different, for one thing.

22. IPSWICH, MASSACHUSETTS. There is unchanging charm in the two greens of this gracious town.

Eighteenth-century houses used to smell of furniture polished with beeswax and turpentine, of rugs swept with wet tea leaves, of newly baked bread, and candle smoke. Timothy Dexter was awakened in the morning by the sound and scent of coffee being ground. After that he would smell three kinds of hot bread baking and a steak sizzling over the red coals of a wood fire. What he would say if he woke up tomorrow and inhaled the modern aroma of bath salts, cigarette butts of five popular brands, and soluble coffee is best left to the imagination.

Fingertips find changes too from year to year. The old furniture was pine, smoothed and waxed and polished, but the newer mahogany always felt smoother and glassier. The roughness of handwoven wool and linen of the seventeenth century has given place to the softness of brocade and satin. Instead of the slightly greasy feel of pewter, there is the cold hardness of silver. Floors grow slippery; rugs, soft. It is no longer necessary to scald your fingers on a hot tea cup: the new ones have handles and light shows through the plates, if you hold them up to the window. The thick brown and buff bowls have been put into the shed chamber along with great grandfather's tavern table. The new punch bowl rings like a bell when it is touched by the silver ladle.

We can see the earlier simpler furniture of the seventeenth century against its proper background in the Whipple House at Ipswich. Built about 1640 this is one of the oldest houses in the state, the type with the huge central chimney and with an overhanging second story on the gable end. At Ipswich there are two greens—the North Green and the South Green. The town was a frontier settlement when the beams for the Whipple House were being hewn but it was also a literary center. Its most famous citizen in this early time was Nathaniel Ward, who wrote *The Simple Cobbler of Aggawam*. Ward took a pessimistic view of life and his simple cobbler was an attempt to prove that it was impossible for a man to live in New England by the labor of his own hands.

Samuel Sewall took a brighter view of the region that he

and Ward both knew and he gives an attractive picture of how it must have seemed to dwellers near the greens of Ipswich. The Devil is supposed to have left his footprint near the North Green but he seems, according to Sewall's account, to have departed and left the place in peace.

As long as Plum Island shall faithfully keep the commanded Post, notwithstanding the hectoring words and hard blows of the proud and boisterous ocean; . . . as long as any Cattell shall be fed with the Grass growing in the meadows . . .; As long as any Sheep shall walk upon Old-town Hills, and shall thence pleasantly look down upon . . . the fruitful marishes lying beneath; As long as any free and harmless Doves shall find a White oak . . . to perch, feed, or build a careless nest upon . . .; As long as nature shall constantly remember to give the rows of Indian Corn their education by pairs—so long shall Christians be born there and . . . be made partakers of the Saints of Light.

From the South Green at Ipswich it is less than a mile to the town wharf where you can hire a boat for Plum Island and see for yourself whether Sewall's prophecy still holds.

On Byfield Green which contains the campus of Governor Dummer Academy, stands the only haunted house we know. Few New England houses have even one ghost but Governor Dummer's mansion has at least three. One of them is the ghost of a white horse. Governor Dummer rode it up the staircase on the night of the housewarming in 1715 and continues to do so on the night of the first full moon whenever August has two of them. Occasionally the ghost of an English officer is seen wandering about the place in periwig, lace ruffles, and embroidered cloak. He is still carrying the sword that was in his hand when he was killed in a duel.

The third ghost has been laid. For many years a small child, always smiling, peeped into the kitchen through the same door. In making some repairs, workmen found a child's ring in a crack in the floor near the place where she used to stand. Below in the cellar was found a box containing a child's bones. They were buried in the graveyard and the gentle little ghost vanished. The handsome house on Byfield Green must miss her.

23. BILLERICA, MASSACHUSETTS. This green and village have been developing since the seventeenth century.

CHAPTER 5

Wilderness to Village Green at Billerica

*I*t took a long time for the pattern of the village green as we now know it to emerge. We think of it with the white spire of a meetinghouse rising against the sky, with fine old trees casting shadows on neatly mown grass, and a frame of gleaming houses and fences. The whole seems withdrawn from the bustle of life—peaceful, orderly.

Yet behind the safe, quiet villages are many stories of danger and violence. In the seventeenth century these were frontier settlements. The wilderness lay just beyond and the shadows that flitted through the trees were bears, catamounts, wolves, or worse still, Indians. Indeed, there are few villages that do not have a history of women dragged into captivity, houses put to the torch, men scalped and killed.

Today we so often see white towns centered on well-kept greens that we assume the first settlers had the picture clearly in mind. Actually their pattern was quite different from the one that developed and which we now see. True the idea of the safely enclosed green space was the same, but the buildings that formerly surrounded it looked quite different. The earlier structures had an Elizabethan air with their diamond-paned casements, overhanging upper stories, and many-gabled roofs. The men who laid out the seventeenth-century greens in New England had memories of English villages of an even earlier time.

The furnishings of the houses were also reminiscent of days gone by. Chairs were still seats of honor for elders. Young people and children sat on benches or stools. The dining table was a wide board. It stood against the wall when not in use and rested on trestles during the meals. These trestle tables have usually been considered space-saving devices, but there is also the possibility that both in English castles and the houses of the American wilderness a strong board was a valuable shield in times of attack. As in Elizabethan England, early American households treasured a few pieces of pewter for the table, but horn cups and wooden trenchers were in more general use.

Just now we are writing at a table made of a pine board seven feet long and thirty inches wide. The father and mother who once sat at its head and foot each had an English pewter plate but their eight children ate from a wooden trencher that ran almost the length of the table and held eight portions of whatever there was for dinner. If the smaller boys left some bear meat or hasty pudding, it was soon disposed of by an older brother with hollow legs.

There were silver teaspoons for company, but the children used pewter spoons which they themselves made in a mold. The process is not difficult. We have made some ourselves and are sometimes mistakenly congratulated on having such a large number of antique pewter spoons. We have some of the old silver ones, too. One of them was rescued from a pigpen a hundred years ago and still shows the marks of a hog's teeth. Our table was forgotten in a Vermont attic for half a century until we rescued it and scraped away the red paint. It has outlasted many others made since and is good for—how many centuries more?

Like the houses around the early commons our table, even when it was new, belonged to a still older way of living. It

took a long time for the designs of Chippendale and Sheraton to reach country cabinetmakers in the hill towns of New
England. Eighteenth-century master builders, who brought to
village greens Doric pediments, modillions, dentil cornices,
leaded fanlights, and the shining whiteness of pillars and clapboards, were adding something new to a picture that now
looks very old.

This evolution from a frontier settlement in a primeval
forest to the village green we see today is plainly visible in
the town of Billerica. We might have chosen some other town
to illustrate the change—the story is repeated many times—
but we feel at home in Billerica. The names on the old gravestones are familiar to us, the mirror over our hall table hung
in a house there two hundred years ago, and it was from
Billerica that our great grandfather went forth to fight the
British at Lexington. Besides Billerica's green has a proper
feeling: it touches both past and present. The roads that di-
verge from the triangle under the elms are busy ones, but
there is a withdrawn and peaceful air about the square houses,
the pillared white church, even the shops, and the bandstand
on the green. Looking at it now, we find it difficult to realize
that this quiet town evolved from an untenanted wilderness.

During the first thirty years of its existence the Massachusetts Colony planted, as the saying was, thirty-one towns. As
early as 1635, there was talk of a settlement at Shaweshin—
one way of spelling the Indian name for what is now Billerica
—and in 1642 land was granted there to the church at Cambridge. No distinction between church and town was made in
the different agreements which assumed that the church at
Cambridge and the town of Cambridge were the same. So
they were, and originally Billerica belonged to both. Then in
1654 fourteen men, living in what had recently been a forest,
petitioned the General Court to change the name of the town
from Shaweshin to Billericay. The court granted the request
but in its statement there was already an indication of spelling difficulties, "the name of the plantation to be called Bil-
lerikeyca." Today there is a hint of the old spelling in the

pronunciation which cannot be exactly indicated. To master it, you must simply go there and listen.

In 1655 Billerica was incorporated and became like other towns in New England and like the colony itself, a miniature republic, compact, unified, with enough power and vitality to support both a religious and a civil government. Citizenship depended on church membership, a narrow and exclusive policy perhaps, but it guaranteed that new settlers would not be merely restless adventurers but groups bound by ties of family and religion.

From the first, common land was part of the Billerica town plan. Herds were kept in common and the cowherds were paid by each owner according to the number of his cattle, which, it was agreed, might be "driven over Concord River when the water is low, that the catell may pass through the river."

We like to imagine how they looked on some September day when the water was low at the ford: the cows, red, brindled, brown, splashing through the shallows under swamp maples already turning crimson and plum; behind them a sunburned, tousle-headed, gangling boy in brown homespun, a gun under his arm, a powder horn across his shoulder. He would use his gun chiefly for prodding an adventurous heifer back into line, but he might need it for their protection too. Wolves were still so common that in 1661 rewards were offered for them. The cowherd knows that "what person so ever shall kill a wolfe shall have for every wolfe killed and brought to the constable accordinge to law twenty shillings . . . provided that either English or Indian shall make proof to the constable that it was killed within the bounds of the Towne."

The town fathers planned for the comfort as well as the safety of the cattle. In laying out roads around the common, they marked groups of trees for survival so that the cows could rest in their shade. It was considerations of safety, however, that most affected the appearance of the growing village. In 1667 the General Court ordered all towns to erect some sort of fortification where women and children could be guarded in time of danger. It was suggested that the meeting-houses be fortified. The houses built at the time already had some protection in overhanging second stories. Again we trace a connection between these American houses subject to Indian attack and earlier dwellings in England, where in Chester, for instance, you still walk along arcades made by the projecting upper stories of houses built in defense of the wild Welsh who came out of the mountains, battered at the doors, and were driven off by a downpouring of hot lead.

It was in 1675 that Billerica prepared for trouble. The Indians under King Philip that year made a determined effort to wipe out the white men. Swansea, Brookfield, Deerfield, Hadley, Springfield, Lancaster, Groton, Medfield, Wey-mouth, and Marlborough were all savagely attacked. Although many of these places are widely separated according to travel at the time, the Indians seemed to be everywhere at once and the ashes of one town were hardly cold before flames broke out in another.

Billerica resolved in a town meeting held in June that:

The Towne, considering the providence of God at the present call-ing us to lay aside our ordinary occations in providing for our crea-tures and to take special care for the preserving of our lives and the lives of our wives and children, the enemy being near and the warn-ing by gods providence upon our neighbors being very solemne and awfull, do therefore order & agree joyntly to prepare a place of safety for women and children . . .

Eight houses were chosen for garrisons and those assigned to garrison duty were ordered to leave all other work and make the house ready for defence. Brush and underwood were ordered cleared away from each garrison and the in-habitants were told to "attend their severall watches, as for-merly, untill further order."

Eleven soldiers and six families were assigned to the house of the minister, Mr. Whiting, and this was "to bee ye maine garrison and last refuge in case of extremity." We have seen a photograph of one of these old Billerica garrisons which was still standing not far from the common, sixty years ago. It was about thirty feet across the front with a lean-to at the back making the end dimension on the ground almost as long. Unpainted with twenty small panes to a window and built around a central chimney, it had probably four rooms downstairs and as many above, besides an attic with one very small window. To this house were assigned four families—which contributed five soldiers—and two soldiers of the militia. Youthful enthusiasm was checked by the order that "every p'son that shall shoot off a gun, small or great, without leave from a commander, shall pay a fine of two shillings and sixpence, or set off so much of their wages, if they be garrison men."

Actually Billerica suffered no serious damage during this period when it was conquering the wilderness and taking precautions against attack. It probably escaped because of good relations with the local redmen who were some of John Eliot's praying Indians. Through Eliot, their sachem, Passaconway, was friendly toward the settlers. When he was dying, he warned his people "to take heed how they quarrelled with their English neighbors, for though they might do them damage, yet it would prove the means of their own destruction."

Passaconway's son, Wannalancet, followed his father's advice. Instead of joining Philip, he withdrew his tribe into the forests of New Hampshire. At the end of the war, he visited the minister at Chelmsford, near Billerica, to ask if the town had suffered during the fighting.

The clergyman said that it had not, "Thanks be to God."

"Me next," said Wannalancet.

The Indian assault so long guarded against in Billerica, came finally in 1692 when two women, each with two children, were killed by the savages. Three years later came a second attack on a section of the town without garrisons. The Indians came suddenly in the daytime. A man who was taking his noonday rest was shot in the neck by an arrow. He pulled it out and died with it in his hand. A badly wounded woman threw herself out of a window, hid among some plants, and escaped death. Another was scalped and left for dead, but lived. Children were killed and captured. The inhabitants pursued the Indians but never caught them. There is a tradition that the savages tied up the mouths of the dogs with wampum so that they could not bark and show which way their masters had gone. These assaults were episodes in what was known as King William's war, which lasted for ten years.

The greens of New England have their peaceful atmosphere today because of the crowded garrison houses of a century ago, because of men sweating through swamps and forests and doing their herding and haying with arms at hand. And the women also did their part. They did not confine themselves entirely to spinning and cooking. There is a story in the Law family of one afternoon in the year 1704 when their garrison house in Billerica was left with only one man on guard. The daughter, Mary, looking out of the window, noticed a stump at the edge of the woods. She thought it moved and urged the guard to shoot at it. When he laughed at her, she seized his gun and fired at the stump and hit it. A dead Indian rolled over.

The compactness of New England villages like Billerica has resulted from an early mutual need for protection. So has the New England tradition of neighborliness, a spirit necessary in times of danger and useful in peaceful pursuits— the building of houses, the raising of barns and meeting-houses, even the making of quilts.

Billerica's first meetinghouse was built in 1658. It was a small structure, covered with boards outside and with a thatched roof. Later a gallery was added and shingles substituted for thatch. In this form it was used for almost forty years. Then it was decided to build a larger one. All persons capable of labor in Billerica were summoned to appear at seven o'clock in the morning "at the second beat of the drumb." Men came to help from other towns too—arrangements were made for their dinner—and on the third day the work was finished, "not a bone broken and we concluded with a psalm of praise."

The third meetinghouse was built in 1737. It was even larger and had a bell brought from England. No matter what the size of the building, nor the time of its completion, the same problem inevitably arose: who should sit in the choice places? A committee was appointed to assign seats and to hear complaints about decisions, but there was no democratic nonsense about the apportioning. Differences of wealth, rank, and social position were recognized even among the hard-working yeomen of Billerica and there was room for jealousy among their wives. Aggrieved ladies often appealed to the selectmen and at such times, to the seating committee, an Indian war whoop must have been remembered as a pleasant sound!

The fourth meetinghouse was built in 1797. It originally looked north but later was turned to face east, as it does today. The common it faced at Billerica must have looked then much as it does at present. The meetinghouse and fine square houses near it cannot have changed a great deal. The new church—this one of 1797—was built by Ephraim Kidder. It has a graceful steeple, a simple but well-designed cornice, and finely proportioned pillars. The steeple, with its clock and gold-pennant weather vane, is another good illustration of the different ways Yankee carpenters solved the problem of the spire. We have spoken of the elaborate treatment of the steeple of Park Street Church in Boston. At Billerica the transition from four-sided clock tower to eight-sided spire is solved more simply but still most pleasingly. The clock tower has a square railing. Inside this is a square structure with eight arched windows which lead the eye naturally to an octagonal railing above and so to the eight windows of the third stage. On this is set the spire itself, also octagonal, but tapering gracefully to a final sharp point.

The steeple is beautiful to gaze upon but it makes us shudder to think of working at such a height. Among the few occupations that never attracted us at any time is that of steeple jack. In reading the Billerica records, we discovered that our apprehensiveness was well founded for the Billerica steeple once collapsed. It fell and the builder of it was given five hundred dollars. The payment puzzles us. We should think the builder would have had to pay a forfeit. However, we are glad that he was so well treated and that he was not killed. If he had, we should not be sitting here comfortably writing about him a hundred and fifty years later for he was one of our great great grandfathers and though one has a large number, the set has to be complete or one turns out to be someone else.

The names of the pew owners in the meetinghouse of Billerica are the same as those on the rolls of the soldiers of the Revolution—French, Kidder, Pollard, Barret, Kittredge—most of them familiar in the town since its first settlement. There is no memorial to them on the green, the green itself is their monument. The names of the men who died in the Civil War may be read on a granite column which carries on top a delightfully unmilitary looking soldier. With his walrus moustache, baggy trousers, billowing coat, like a comfortable dressing gown, and his casual way of leaning on his musket, he might be a Mauldin character of a century ago.

Near the monument are pyramids of old cannon balls. One day as we walked across the green a small blue-bonneted girl was trying to push one about, while her mother rested at the foot of the Second World War monument. On the ground, near the Honor Roll of the Second World War, a soldier of it lay asleep, with yellow elm leaves drifting down over him. We wondered which of the thousand names on the board was his. Some were Anglo-Saxon like those on the old records; others, like the names on all Honor Rolls, remind us that this war was fought by Americans of many racial strains.

Their names are different from those of the founders of the town. They worship in many churches and the bandstand rather than the meetinghouse may draw them to the common now. Yet they have an essential kinship with the early settlers who hewed common out of wilderness. No one—man or woman—who was soft survived that life. Again, in a different sort of trial, the old spirit of independence, ingenuity, and grit has proved its existence again. Village greens, those links between present and past, are, indeed, the proper place for the recording.

CHAPTER *6*

Lexington Green, Nibor Muzzy's Land

*A*t Lexington we live American history; we do not simply remember it. Indeed so vivid are our thoughts as our gaze travels over the broad triangle that Lexington's Battle Green is *the* green, the most typical and symbolic one of all.

AT A PUBLIC MEETING IN
1707 A COMMITTEE WAS
CHOSEN TO TREAT WITH
"NIBOR MUZZY"
ABOUT THE PURCHASE OF
A PIECE OF LAND FOR
PUBLIC USE
FOUR YEARS LATER
FOR £16
HE DEEDED THE INHABITANTS
THIS SPOT
"FOR THE COMMON USE OF ALL"

Perhaps we think in this way of the piece of land that once belonged to "Nibor Muzzy"—as the tablet states—because it follows so closely the pattern of how a green should look.

It is all there: the smoothly mown triangle of green grass, the airy fountains of elms, the beautiful old houses, still used and still lovingly spread with white paint, the meetinghouse with classic portico and tapering spire with a flash of gold at the top, and the tavern near by. These are the familiar elements, but at Lexington there is something more—a direct contact with the far-reaching events of the Revolution.

Henry Hudson Kitson's statue of the Minuteman does more than commemorate a great day. It symbolizes an enduring quality—the courage which Emerson defined as being "adequate to the emergency." The Minuteman stands with a spirited, careless adequacy as appropriate to aviators or paratroopers in olive drab as to those men in linsey woolsey and butternut-dyed shirts who assembled on Lexington Green before dawn on the nineteenth of April, 1775.

If the soldiers who faced the British on that spring morning could walk on the green today, they would find it both changed and familiar. They would notice that the Marrett-Munroe House, which some of them had known for almost fifty years, has a different roof line at the back. The roof used to slope all the way down from the third story to the ground. Perhaps as small boys some of them had climbed that long expanse and slid gleefully down. Now the slope is shortened. It changes its direction to cover a porch and the slide is spoiled.

If they could find it, they would recognize the belfry from which sounded the alarm on the fateful morning. It stands southwest of the green on a little hill where it always stood, but is not visible from the green now because of intervening buildings. They might not realize that the present structure is a faithful copy, not original, but they would certainly miss the old bell that summoned them to meeting, rang out the curfew at night, and counted out in solemn strokes the ages of those who died. It disappeared many years ago.

New to them would be many of the buildings, even the meetinghouse. Perhaps this would not seem strange, the town needed a new meetinghouse, but they would certainly be

24. LEXINGTON, MASSACHUSETTS. The green wakes up every nineteenth of April.

aroused when they visited the Memorial Building and studied the picture of the battle painted by Henry Sandham. Probably no battle looks the same to any two men. Certainly there are as many versions of the Battle of Lexington as there are artists. The earliest prints show the Americans throwing down their arms and running away from the British fire, but as the years go on the Americans stand with more and more martial poise. (It was a Concord man who called this development to our attention.)

If the visitors from another century would walk a short distance from the green, they would recognize the old Hancock-Clarke House and remember that John Hancock and Samuel Adams slept there on the night of the eighteenth. Among the treasures of the house they might find some familiar faded silk dress or embroidered waistcoat. Certainly they would recognize the drum, for it was the one beaten at the battle. The sight of it would bring back the sound of it and also the squeaking of Jonathan Harrington's fife. This was the younger Jonathan Harrington, who survived the battle, and always spoke of himself as the Minuteboy, even when he was ninety-four years old.

They would remember the beautiful Georgian doorway of the older Jonathan Harrington's house and recall the moment when he dragged himself across the green to die at his wife's feet. They would recognize the old stones in the burying ground too; only their own names and those of their friends would look strange.

The roof of the Buckman Tavern would not be familiar but inside they would feel at home because the rooms are much as they were when, as Minutemen, they used to refresh themselves there after drilling on the green. They might remember the old flip glasses on the tavern table and recall too the mixed emotions with which they left the big fireplace and straggled out to line up on the green that morning of the nineteenth.

Because we think of Paul Revere's ride in Longfellow's words, we have the feeling that *A voice in the darkness, a knock at the door* came as a complete surprise *to every Middlesex village and farm.* As a matter of fact, the colonists had known for a long time that the British were likely to try to destroy the military stores at Concord. Revere's definite information about the time the British left Boston and the route they were taking was of great value, but the element of surprise was small.

Long before Revere started on his ride, a party of cloaked horsemen rode through Lexington. Their cloaks blew aside as they took the Concord Road and they were recognized as armed British officers. These were the men who later captured Revere and thought they had kept the news from getting through to Concord. They did not count on Dr. Prescott's staying late courting and later still riding on to warn Concord. Neither did it occur to the British that their party would be as conspicuous on the road to Lexington as a full-rigged ship on a millpond. With calm indifference to the yokels they met, they rode on, satisfied that their cloaks were cloaks of invisibility, but the men they had passed soon put the news into circulation and prepared to defend their position. They were a shabbily clad group compared to the soldiers they faced, although at least one of them—so his great granddaughter told us—had a new suit. Around noon on the eighteenth this young minuteman rushed home to announce to his mother that there would be a battle with the regulars soon, probably the next day.

His mother's reaction was natural—to a New Englander. "John," she said, "you haven't a thing fit to wear."

"What's the matter with what I have on?" inquired her son, but his mother insisted that he was not going to meet the uniformed regulars in patched breeches and with his sleeves halfway up his arms.

"Go out to the pasture and shear me a white sheep and a black one," she ordered. So John caught the sheep and sheared them. When he brought in the fleeces, the women of the family had all gathered—his mother, grandmother, sisters, aunts. They washed the wool, carded, and spun it.

The warp was all ready on the loom and as fast as the wool was spun, his mother wove it. Then the women cut out the coat and breeches, basted, fitted, sewed seams, made buttonholes, sewed on buttons.

By the time the British arrived, John, in a neat pepper-and-salt suit and freshly laundered shirt, was attired to meet them.

Until that morning, Lexington's history had been much like that of the other towns around it. Up to 1712 it had been part of Cambridge. It was known as Cambridge Farms and the people of Cambridge cut hay and chopped wood there. Although it never suffered from Indian attacks, it sent a number of men to the French and Indian wars and those same men who had fought for the British became part of the militia that fought against them.

In reading the records of Lexington in Revolutionary times, and those of other New England towns, we were surprised to see how well, in spite of the difficulties of communication, the people were informed about the issues involved in the conflict with England. Without telephone or radio, with only casual postal service, with few newspapers, the farmers and mechanics of New England towns quickly learned that the measures taken by the British government endangered their rights as Englishmen. Again and again the resolutions passed in the meetinghouses on the village greens affirmed the people's loyalty to the king but also their determination to uphold rights guaranteed them by Magna Carta and by their own colonial charters.

To maintain these rights the people of Lexington resolved, "to sacrifice our estates and everything dear in life, yes life itself, in support of the common cause." It was a convenient slogan—no taxation without representation—as easy for us to understand as it was for them, but the colonists realized too, what we seldom hear mentioned today, that in handing over cases of tax violations to the admiralty courts, where no juries were used, the government was threatening the right of trial by jury.

The people understood because their ministers understood. Resolutions passed in town meetings were often drawn up by the ministers. The system by which Massachusetts permitted a town to incorporate only after a minister had been established to preach now bore fruit. In many New England pulpits there were educated, intelligent men who knew and said that the question was not one of taxes but of freedom. In Lexington, the Rev. Jonas Clarke played a significant part in helping the town prepare for its great day. Indeed, it was at his door that Paul Revere knocked to inform Hancock and Adams that the regulars were on the march.

The darkness had not yet lifted when Captain John Parker called out his company of minutemen. Perhaps the best account of the events on the Battle Green comes from his famous grandson, Theodore Parker:

The war of the Revolution began at Lexington to end at Yorktown. Its first battle was on the 19th of April. In the raw morning a little after daybreak, a tall man with a large forehead under a three cornered hat, drew up his company of seventy men on the green: farmers and mechanics like himself. Only one is left now (1851) the boy Jonathan Harrington, the fifer who played the men to the spot.

They wheeled into line to wait for the regulars. The Captain ordered every man to load his piece with powder and ball.

'Stand your ground. Don't fire,' were his words, 'unless you are fired upon, but if they want a war, let it begin here.'

The regulars came on. Some Americans offered to run away from their post.

Captain Parker said: 'I will order the first man shot who leaves this place.' The English commander (Pitcairn) cried out: 'Disperse, you rebels! Lay down your arms and disperse.' Not a man stirred. 'Disperse, you damned rebels!' shouted he again. Not a man stirred. He ordered the vanguard to fire. They did but over the heads of our fathers. Then the whole main body levelled their pieces and there was need of ten new graves in Lexington. A few Americans returned the shot. British blood stained the grass.

'Disperse and take care of yourselves,' was the Captain's last command. There lay the dead and there stood the soldiers. There was a battlefield between England and America, never to be forgot, never to be covered over.

The meeting on Lexington green delayed Major Pitcairn and his troops only half an hour. Yet as he marched on to Concord, bells were ringing in his ears from meetinghouses all over the countryside, stirring Yankee blood. From Lancaster, Leominster, Chelmsford, Carlisle, Billerica, Brookline, Reading, Needham and other towns, men hurried towards Lexington through the hot spring morning. New England ploughs were left standing in fields while their owners rode the plough horses toward Boston.

In Leominster one young man, Joshua White, was out on the pond with two ladies. David Wilder, who wrote the history of the town, says that White heard the alarm guns being shot off on the common and that, without his realizing it, the boat drifted so near the dam that all he could do was to head the bow straight and let it go over, an event which occasioned this poetical outburst from a local pen:

> *But White being strong and meeting no harm*
> *He took a Miss Wheelock under each arm*
> *And carried both safely ashore,*
> *Then bid them good bye and said nothing more;*
> *But hurried home and snatched his gun*
> *And went to fight at Lexington.*

In these circumstances it took a Yankee to say good-by and "nothing more."

Joshua White and the other men who snatched up guns and powder horns that morning soon learned not to face the British fire in a body but to rely on lessons they had learned from the Indians, using stone walls, fences, and trees for cover. When Pitcairn led his troops back towards Boston after the fight at the bridge in Concord, it was the soldiers in the scarlet coats who were the targets. The Americans in their home-dyed homespuns were well camouflaged. They melted into the shadows of pines, into piles of rails and brush. Now they chose the targets and proved on the Battle Road through Lincoln that they could hit them.

Captain Parker rallied his men to avenge the losses of the morning. This time their fire did damage. The real battle of Lexington began and soon the British retreat became a rout. The dead and many of the wounded lay where they fell. As the British troops passed Lexington Green again, weary, dirty, thirsty, almost out of ammunition, they were, an English writer says, "driven before the Americans like sheep."

It was only the arrival of reinforcements led by Lord Percy that saved Pitcairn's troops from destruction. It is even said that Pitcairn would have surrendered if he could have found a general officer to whom to give up his sword. Percy's brigade formed a hollow square not far from the green to receive the exhausted men who, "were obliged to lie down on the ground, their tongues hanging out of their mouths like dogs after a chase."

Lord Percy did not waste much time attacking the rebels. He contented himself with shooting one or two cannon balls into the town of Lexington. One went through the meeting-house window and lodged on the green. Lately it has been the fashion to speak of the Battle of Lexington as an unimportant skirmish—"Concord supplied the ground and Acton the men"—but Percy's own account of it showed that it had a significance beyond the success or failure of the British attack on Concord. He wrote:

The whole country was covered with stone walls and was besides a very hilly, stony country. We retired for fifteen miles under an incessant fire, which like a moving circle followed us wherever we went till we arrived at Charlestown at 8 in the evening . . . having exhausted almost every cartridge. You will easily conceive that in such a retreat and harassed as we were on all sides, it was impossible not to lose a good many men.

During the whole affair the Rebels attacked us in a very scattered, irregular manner but with perseverance and resolution. Nor did they ever dare to form into a regular body. Indeed they knew too well what was proper to do so.

Whoever looks upon them as an irregular mob will find himself much mistaken . . . nor will the insurrection here turn out so despicable as it is perhaps imagined at home. For my part, I never believed, I confess, that they would have attacked the king's troops or have had the perseverance I found they showed yesterday.

The British losses in killed, wounded, and missing were two hundred and seventy-three against ninety-three on the American side. For those who consider the battles of Lexington and Concord minor skirmishes, it is perhaps worth noting that the British losses were larger than at the admittedly important battle on the Plains of Abraham where Canada was won and Montcalm and Wolfe fell.

Earl Percy, on the first day of the Revolutionary War, formed a just estimate of these men who had been drilled on the village greens. Indeed, their insurrection was not to prove despicable. Samuel Adams, that morning had also correctly estimated the importance of the day. He and Hancock were persuaded by their friends to leave the Clarke house for some safer place.

"What a glorious morning!" Adams panted as they hurried across the field. His friend, surprised at having the weather, that favorite New England topic, discussed just then, politely replied, "Yes, but very warm for the time of year."

"I meant," said Adams, "what a glorious morning for America."

On all but one day of the year the green at Lexington is a quiet place. Elms and maples come into full leaf and make deep pools of shade and turn scarlet and gold. In autumn the grass is soft and thick and very green with a scatter of bright leaves over it. They are raked up and blue smoke rises as they burn. Later snow falls on the Minuteman and covers the boulder on which Captain Parker's words are cut. Elm branches are sharp against the sky. Boys throw snow balls and forget that Lafayette and Washington came there to shake the hands of men who heard Parker's words on the battle day; forget the wounded Jonathan Harrington dragging himself to his door; forget the British soldiers with their tongues hanging out and their faces redder than their coats; forget even the sound of a horse galloping through the night.

Then suddenly some morning, there is a soft green haze on the elms and Lexington's great day is again at hand. Some years the elms are in leaf and the fruit trees are in bloom, as they were on the day of battle. Yet even if April snow falls, the town wakes up on the nineteenth.

The green is crowded with people. There are minutemen and British soldiers. The young man in black with the laced shirt and riding the chestnut horse, which looks willing to jump over a stone wall any minute, is Dr. Prescott.

At last, far down the Cambridge road come shouts and then hoof beats.

"Was it like this the day of the battle, Grandmamma?" inquires our small granddaughter, for we have described it with such enthusiasm that she is sure we were there in 1775.

"It's the way it is now because of the way it was then," we say as we both watch Paul Revere gallop up to the statue and rein in his horse on Lexington Green.

25. BOSTON, MASSACHUSETTS. For three hundred years the Common has
been the heart of the city.

CHAPTER 7

"That Beloved Place," the Common

*I*f Lexington has the Green, Boston has the Common. For more than three hundred years it has been the heart of the city and to a New Englander the Common always means Boston Common. There our sense of the past is keenest. Down the wide mall under the elms move many familiar shadows. There is genial Oliver Wendell Holmes, just having finished perhaps one of those sprightly papers about the Autocrat of the Breakfast Table. There is Longfellow strolling across the Common on his way to his publishers'. They meet and Holmes' remarks make the poet throw back his handsome head and laugh. The sunlight shines on his pink cheeks and silver whiskers. If we loiter along the pleasant paths, Aldrich or Thoreau or Lowell may also pass by.

Not all the authors who walk on the Common are homegrown. That elegantly dressed young man with his glossy hair arranged in ringlets is Charles Dickens. His books are so exciting that Bostonians crowd the dock when a ship is due with another installment of *The History of David Copperfield* to see whether David has at last had the sense to marry Agnes. That tall man with the spectacles is Thackeray;

the loud-voiced, red-faced giant is Trollope. All walk on the Common. Everyone does who comes to Boston.

They would find the Common changed today, but they still would recognize it, even though on Tremont Street subway stations have thrust their way out of the earth and on the Beacon Street side the State House has grown an outsize pair of wings. If they should inquire about this curious architectural calamity, they would learn that it might have been worse. When the idea of enlarging the State House was under consideration, one of the legislators' friends who happened to own a marble quarry, brought in a bill specifying that the wings should be of marble and should harmonize with the Bulfinch front. To the quarry owner this seemed inappropriate. He suggested a simple amendment involving the change of only a few words: the Bulfinch front should harmonize with the new wings. At the last minute Boston architects discovered the amendment and aroused enough public indignation to defeat it. So when we look at the old red bricks of the handsome Bulfinch building, we can be grateful they are not veneered with white marble.

The Common is now, as it has been for the half century, a space that starts out to be rectangular and then, with true Boston independence, changes its mind. Charles Street, its western boundary; Beacon Street on the north, Park Street on the east make three sides of the rectangle. Tremont Street on the south makes a long diagonal and Boylston makes a shorter one to meet Charles Street again.

Originally set aside by Governor Winthrop as a training field and cow pasture, the Common still shows traces of both activities. It is claimed that cows are responsible for the aimless paths that never seem to lead where you wish to go. Perhaps this is true, but it is easier to trace the connection with the training field. Only a short time ago young men bound for war marched on the Common and the U. S. O. buildings where so many soldiers and sailors were welcomed are still standing.

Like other village greens in New England, Boston Common also has its monument to the men who died for the preservation of the union, a tall shaft on a high knoll. The Common has, in fact, almost every feature we expect to find on or near a village green—a framed Honor Roll of the recent war, a bandstand, a fountain, even a graveyard where old stones close to the roar of Tremont Street traffic seem as remote as if they were on some country hillside.

The Common has its meetinghouse, too, for Park Street Church rises above the trees at one corner on what was once part of the Common. When Bostonians agree to meet "in front of Stearns's," it is the clock on Park Street Church that tells if they are on time. We have an old geography from which children in 1830 memorized a list of the tall buildings of the world. The list included the Pyramids of Giza, Strasbourg Cathedral, and—number six—Park Street Church in Boston.

A typical feature of village greens that is missing from the Common is the tavern, but the Parker House is close by where wonderful oysters and beans and brown bread bring back memories of earlier days. We must also move a short distance from the Common for a library, too often the ugliest building on the village green, but in Boston the Athenaeum, which looks out on Old Granary Burying Ground— once part of the Common—is a dignified and stately example of the architecture of the first half of the nineteenth century. This is a private library, owned by shareholders. It not only has a look of distinction but smells the way an old library should and has the peculiar cool hush that goes with learning—a hush that is revered. We once knew a reader who slipped on the perilous iron stairs and plunged down the whole flight, scattering six volumes of Trollope as she fell. She had scarcely struck the ground at the foot of a disapproving marble statue when two Helen Hokinson characters emerged from the twilight and said "SH!"

On the old paths of the Common the Boston of Holmes and Lowell is only the other day. If we step farther back we can see George Washington, the recently elected president of the United States, waiting to enter the city and ride past the Common. It is a windy day in October but hundreds of school children are lined up to greet him. So is a troop of cavalry and there is a long discussion about which shall go first. Finally, after the horses have almost ridden over the children, it is agreed that the children shall stand in front. (By that time many of them and the bystanders, too, have caught cold in the piercing wind.)

Governor John Hancock has ordered a splendid dinner for the President at the mansion on the Beacon Street side of the Common, but a point of etiquette is involved. The Governor thinks the President should call on him first. Washington knows that the dignity of his office entitles him to be waited upon by Hancock, so he goes to lodgings instead of to the mansion on Beacon Street. Hancock sends a message to say that he is sorry not to be able to call upon the President: he is suffering from an attack of gout. The President regrets the Governor's affliction but remains in his lodgings. At last Hancock gives in. With his leg swathed in bandages, he has himself carried into the President's room by two sturdy men. Washington receives the Governor with courtesy and great sympathy for his ailment.

Some of the unfortunates who are still sneezing from exposure to the Boston wind complain that the Governor got over his gout a good deal sooner than they will recover from their colds.

In 1630 the Common was already an English settlement. It had one inhabitant, William Blaxton, who used to ride a brindled bull around the scrubby fields, among the boulders and blueberry bushes, the swamp holes and trickles of "sweet water." Just how wild the place was is a matter of opinion. One traveler wrote that "the hideous thickets are such that wolves and bears nurse up their young from the sight of all beholders." Another noted that: "A little fencing will secure their cattle from the wolves. The place being bare of woods, they are not troubled by those great annoyances, wolves, rattlesnakes, or mosquitoes."

We suppose that very early there must have been squirrels, ancestors of the present ones portrayed in the cartoons of Francis Dahl who we wish might meet the squirrel we saw on the Common the other day. It was supervising in its own imperious way a drinking fountain at which a sailor paused to refresh himself. Perhaps he did not have a Boston accent. In any case, the squirrel did not care to share the fountain with him and made its anger known by distinguished nasal squeaks, until the sailor meekly turned on the water so the squirrel could drink alone. It did so with great neatness and despatch, chattering arrogantly each time the stream stopped. When it was no longer thirsty, it tolerantly accepted a walnut from us and spun it around in its forepaws, sniffing at it suspiciously. What the investigation revealed, we cannot say, but we were gratified to receive one last patronizing look from this descendent of the early settlers before it went off to deepfreeze the nut for the winter.

Blaxton did not stay long after the arrival of John Winthrop and his Puritan followers but went to live in Rhode Island. He first made it possible, however, for the town of Boston to make one of the best bargains in the history of real estate. Blaxton sold the Common to the city fathers for around one hundred and fifty dollars.

In the early days, part of the Common was granted to individuals, but in 1640 the town decided that thereafter "no land for house plot or garden should be granted out of the common fields." Many years later, when Boston became a city, its charter forbade the sale or lease of any part of the Common. There have been many attempts to sidestep this provision but the Boston Common Society has always staunchly defended the area against encroachments.

Originally there were three ponds on the Common. Only the Frog Pond now remains and this is rather a theoretical pond since the water now comes from a bubbler in the bottom, which is covered with cement. It was once proposed to erect an iron fence around the Frog Pond to keep urchins and dogs at a respectable distance. Just what is a respectable

26. BOSTON, MASSACHUSETTS. Urchins still love the Frog Pond on the Common.

distance for an urchin we do not pretend to know, but at least the fence was not put up. The city is generous with water on hot days and we are glad to see urchins—and their dogs, too—still splashing happily around among the toy boats. Every now and then there is a project to call the Frog Pond something more elegant, such as Crescent Lake, but no name ever proves so satisfactory as the early one of Frog Pond.

Near it for many years stood the Old Elm, a landmark on the Common from the time the Puritans came until 1876, when it was blown down in a storm. At one time it was the habit of women who lived close by to light a fire near the great tree, heat water carried from the pond, and do their washing. Even the residents of Beacon Street had their rugs beaten and shaken on the Common until a law was passed forbidding this sociable practice. Edward Everett Hale lamented the end of this custom in an editorial called "The Last Shake."

Our idea of Boston Common in the early days is one of pastoral charm: cows grazing in the shade of the Old Elm or placidly marking out paths between puddles and boulders, boys fishing where Arlington Street now is, men cutting hay or making bricks or playing cricket, women washing petticoats, or just walking up and down the mall in their best clothes.

Yet it would be a mistake to regard the Common as consecrated only to peaceful pursuits. In 1637, William Schouler was the first man hanged there from a branch of the Old Elm, for a real gallows was not set up until 1644. Margaret Jones was executed on the Common for witchcraft. She had been healing people with simple remedies which, with her touch, were said to have produced magical cures. She was accused of possessing imps. Sometimes the hangman was called upon to deal with books instead of people. Censorship has been a respectable pursuit in Boston since 1651, when William Pynchon's *The Meretricious Price of our Redemption* was publicly burned on the Common.

Duels were fought there, too. In 1728, Benjamin Wood-bridge and Henry Philips, two respectable young merchants, quarrelled at the Royal Exchange Tavern, a place of gaming and drinking. They fought on a July night by moonlight at the foot of the Common. Woodbridge was killed. Philips escaped to France, but died there from remorse, it was said, the next year. It was for Woodbridge that Holme's Schoolmistress dropped a rose and a tear on her first walk with the Autocrat. Of their last stroll, Holmes wrote:

It was in the Common that we were walking. The mall of our Common, you know, has various branches leading from it in different directions. One of these runs down from Joy Street southward across the whole length of the Common to Boylston Street. We called it the long path and were fond of it.

I felt very weak indeed (though of a tolerably robust habit) as we came opposite the head of this path on that morning. I think I tried to speak twice without making myself distinctly audible. At last I got out the question: Will you take the long path with me?—Certainly. —said the schoolmistress,—with much pleasure,—Think,—I said,— before you answer; if you take the long path with me now, I shall interpret it that we are to part no more!—The schoolmistress stepped back with a sudden movement as if an arrow had struck her. One of the long granite blocks used as seats was hard by,—the one you may still see, close by the gingko tree—Pray, sit down,—I said. No, no, she answered softly, I will walk the *long path* with you!

English visitors often found that Boston Common reminded them of home. One describes it as "a small but pleasant Common, where the gallants, a little before sunset, walk with their marmalet-madams, as we do in Morefields, till the nine o'clock bell rings them home to their respective habitations. When presently the constables walk their rounds to see good order kept and take up the people."

The reference to Morefields is interesting. It was a place for public recreation near London and made by draining swamp land. Samuel Pepys speaks of walking there. In the eighteenth century an attempt was made to fence it in for private use, but with loud cries of "Shovels and spades!

Shovels and spades!" the angry inhabitants gathered and knocked down the fence as soon as it was set up—an English example of devotion to the principle of land set aside for the common use of all.

Another Englishman, a Mr. Bennett, writes of how the eighteenth-century Common appeared to him:

Every afternoon after drinking tea, the gentlemen and ladies walk the mall, and from thence adjourn to one another's houses to spend the evening. What they call the mall is a walk on a fine green Common . . . It is near half a mile over with two rows of fine young trees . . . with a five foot way between, in imitation of St. James's Park, and part of the Bay of the sea which encircles the town . . . forms a beautiful canal in view of the walk . . . The ladies visit, drink tea, and indulge in every piece of gentility to the height of the mode, and neglect the affairs of their families with as good a grace as the first ladies of London.

This period of aristocratic splendor was brief. Soon the Common was playing a part in the Revolution. It was the scene of many protests against British tyranny. Children would run along the paths shouting "Liberty! Property! No Stamps!" When the Stamp Act was repealed, a pyramid on the Common displayed patriotic paintings illuminated by two hundred and eighty lamps. John Hancock treated everyone to Madeira wine and fireworks were set off. There were rockets, beehives, serpents, and wheels. Sixteen dozen serpents in the air ended the show.

Soon the Common was covered with the white tents of British regiments sent to keep order in Boston. Yet it was still a playground for the boys of the town. They played ball, as they do today, and when there was snow, they brought out their sleds to coast. Once they complained to General Gage that their slides had been destroyed by his soldiers. When the general asked who sent them there to exhibit rebellion, they replied:

Nobody sent us, Sir. We have never insulted your troops, but they have been spoiling our slides. We complained and they called us

27. BOSTON, MASSACHUSETTS. The Ancient and Honorable Artillery Company still parades on the Common before its annual drumhead election of officers.

Young Rebels and told us to help ourselves if we could, and laughed at us. Yesterday our slides were destroyed once more and we will bear it no longer.

There was liberty in the air they breathed, the general concluded, and could not help admiring their spirit. He assured them that in future no one should interfere with their slides. Just where those were we do not know but the slope down from the State House is the steepest and the boys may have sledded there.

When peace with Britain was announced, bells rang out over the Common and cannon were discharged all day. The Governor's House was illuminated and a grand exhibit of fireworks was displayed "such as were never before equalled in this place."

After the war, it continued to be the custom for the militia to parade and manoeuvre on the Common. On such days, "the lower classes divert themselves with such pastimes as suit their particular inclination. A number of tents or temporary booths are put up and furnished with food and liquor for those who require refreshments."

Nathaniel Hawthorne described the scene:

. . . the booths on the Commons, selling ginger-bread, sugar-plums, and confectionery, spruce beer, lemonade. On the top of one of the booths a monkey with a tail two or three feet long. There are boys going about with molasses candy, almost melted down in the sun. Shows: A mammoth rat; a collection of pirates, murderers and the like, in wax. . . .

Today the Ancient and Honorable Artillery Company in full regalia still parades on the Common before its annual drumhead election of officers.

Hawthorne was well aware of the blessings afforded by the open space of green in the midst of the developing city of the early nineteenth century when he wrote:

I went round and across the Common, and stood on the highest point of it, where I could see for miles and miles into the country. Blessed be God for this green tract, and the view which it affords, whereby we poor citizens may be put in mind sometimes that all this earth is not composed of blocks of brick houses and of stone or wooden pavements. Blessed be God for the sky too, though the smoke of the city may somewhat change its aspect—but still it is better than if each street were covered with a roof. There were a good many people walking on the Mall—mechanics apparently, and shopkeepers' clerks with their wives; and boys were rolling on the grass, and I would have liked to lie down and roll too.

A little before the time that Hawthorne felt like rolling on the Common, the town had a conscientious spasm and began to enforce the old laws against Sabbath-breaking. Among other prohibitions was one against bathing at the foot of the Common on Sundays.

A poet was not lacking to comment on this edict:

> In superstitious days, 'tis said,
> Hens laid two eggs on Monday,
> Because a hen would lose her head
> That laid an egg on Sunday.
> Now our wise rulers and the Law
> Say none shall wash on Sunday;
> So Boston folk must dirty go,
> And wash them twice on Monday.

No Boston event, gay or sad, in war or peace, ever seems complete without some contact with the Common. The funeral procession for Alexander Hamilton passed by the Common. The sails of the *Constitution* were made in the old granary near the Common because the spacious floor gave room to spread them out. The Boston Light Infantry lined up at the Common to welcome Commodore Perry. City criers crossed it with bells in their hands announcing Andrew Jackson's victory at New Orleans and triumphant cannon were discharged there.

In 1824, Lafayette passed the Common in a barouche drawn by four white horses and Wendell Phillips stood with the other children waiting for the hero of the Revolution to appear. Many years later Phillips wrote:

I can boast that these eyes have beheld the hero of three revolutions, this hand has touched the right hand that held up Hancock and Washington. I received my first lesson in hero worship. I was so tired after four hours of waiting I could scarcely stand; but when I saw him—that glorious old Frenchman—I could have stood all day.

On that wonderful occasion twenty-five hundred children stood on the Common, the boys in blue coats and white breeches, the girls in white with red ribbons and all carrying bouquets. One six-year-old threw hers in front of the horses that drew the Marquis's carriage. The others followed her example until the street was paved with flowers. As one much farther removed than Phillips from that famous day, we always felt some of the thrill of it when we went to see a certain old lady, a neighbor of ours, who had been kissed by Lafayette. He seems to have shaken all the boys by the hand. Could he have kissed all the girls, too?

Life on Boston Common, however, is not all heroic. Sometimes it is more like life in George Apley's family. Our favorite story of this kind belongs to the Common during the late nineteenth century. Then a pretty and charming young bride, who had the misfortune not to have been born in Boston, came to live on Beacon Hill and no one was ever lonelier.

Years passed, two to be exact, before her horizon brightened and the wife of a business acquaintance of her husband's invited her to a tea. It took courage to accept for she knew no one. When she got home, she still knew no one, except her hostess, who obviously had not known her. However, a lady of forbidding yet benevolent aspect had poured out her tea. Remarks had been exchanged regarding lemon and cream. The east wind had been mentioned. Macaroons had been offered. True, the bride had not been introduced, but she had spoken to a Bostonian and felt that there was someone in the city who would know her if she saw her again.

The very next morning they met on the Common. The

bride received a bow and a kindly smile. She walked home with a warm glow of satisfaction. It had taken awhile, just as people at home had said it would, but now that she at last knew someone, it would not be so bad.

The note that shattered her dream came in the mail the next morning. It read: "I hope you will forgive me for bowing to you and smiling as we met on the Common this morning. Being somewhat nearsighted, I mistook you for some one else. Of course if I had recognized you, I would have smiled, but I would not have bowed."

Perhaps such an incident is possible only on the Common but we never cease to be surprised. The other day in Boston we were getting on a streetcar marked Lechmere. The conductor announced to us, and others, "This car runs to LEECHmere Square. Sometimes pronounced LETCHmere Square, or, by the ultra fastidious, LECKmere Square."

We imagine that people who are exiled from Boston often feel as Benjamin Franklin did in his old age. He remembered how he used to play under the Old Elm and how he used to drive his father's cow home from the Common at sunset. He spoke of it as "that beloved place." Although he could no longer ramble through the city, he still had "a singular pleasure in the company and conversation of its inhabitants . . . The Boston manner, the turn of phrase, and even the tone of voice, and accent and pronunciation all please and refresh me . . ."

Perhaps it was a singular pleasure. People from other parts of the country will think so probably. Bostonians, however, will be happy that one of the truly great men of America carried the speech of Boston in his heart all his days and longed for "that beloved place," the Common.

CHAPTER 8

The Public Garden, Unique Among Village Greens

Ordinarily a city with an open place like the Common in the heart of its busiest section would feel it had devoted enough space to grass and trees and fresh air, but as Boston grew westward, it continued to set aside valuable land for purposes of relaxation. The Public Garden is in a way an extension of the Common. Charles Street, which separates the two is wide and cobbled with heavy trucks rattling down it. Crossing it is an ordeal to the visitor unaccustomed to the city's catch-as-catch-can traffic, but Boston pedestrians are a nimble, hardy, independent lot. Ladies wearing Inverness capes with matching hats and accompanied by Boston terriers, suitably upholstered, dodge imperturbably around the bumpers of trailer trucks.

Perhaps the safest way for the stranger to get from the Common to the Garden is to use one of these matrons as a trail breaker. If he can keep up with her, he will find himself, gasping and slightly dazed at a wrought iron gate where very likely a street photographer will ask if he would like his picture taken. Resisting this temptation, he will enter the Public Garden and find himself in a different world.

Inside the fence is a garden in which Queen Victoria

would have felt at home. A wide walk bordered by formal beds of flowers leads across a miniature suspension bridge, crosses Arlington Street, and connects with the mall on Commonwealth Avenue.

This central path is the main highway of the Garden. Many people use it merely as a pleasant way to get downtown and never turn aside from it. Others with more leisure enjoy the walks that curve away under great beeches or cross by diagonals to smaller gates or lead down to the pond. In the Garden, walks and shrubs, trees, grass, and flowers are all beautifully cared for. Every leaf of the old magnolias seems carefully polished. There is no insincere attempt at naturalness in the Garden. The fountains, the flower beds, the pond, and the islands in it are all frankly and conscientiously artificial and, in spite of being rather like a picture on the stage curtain of a Victorian theater, they achieve an air of elegance, graciousness, and charm.

The change in atmosphere as one crosses Charles Street is far greater than the physical distance would imply. The Common is easy and informal. Men sleep on the grass, the sun shining on their suspender buckles. In the Garden, men wear belts with their trousers; some even wear coats. Those who carry documents in green bags also wear waistcoats. On the Common, newspapers are used to keep the sun out of the eyes of those dozing. Newspapers are read in the Garden and then folded and frugally carried home.

Lovers on the Common are of a forthright type. There are lovers in the Garden, too, but they are more subtle in their ways and can usually be detected only by the quiver of an eyelash. On the Common, there are urchins; in the Garden there are little girls in matching coats and hats in light blue and old rose and jade, young gentlemen who have joined the Navy in very early youth and already have brass buttons and a quarter-deck tone of voice, supercilious pink babies who view the world with a cool blue unwinking gaze from the shelter of broadcloth and mink.

Children do not frequent the Garden in summer. Their

28. BOSTON, MASSACHUSETTS. Thomas Ball's statue of George Washington commands the central path of the Public Garden.

[*137*]

season begins in autumn when elm leaves turn yellow and blow into the water and the young ducklings that held up traffic on Charles Street in the spring are getting large and gawky. Summer seems to stay a little longer in the Garden than it does anywhere else. Grass is cheerfully green there long after it is brown in other places. Scarlet salvias and cannas defy the frost. Crickets keep on chirping there after they are silent in the world outside. The Garden is a trap for sunshine and holds it even when there are cold shadows in the crooked streets downtown.

Even winter seems to touch the Garden gently. The green patina on General Washington's horse stays bright against the snow. The boardwalks on the paths are pleasant underfoot. The sound of skates rings out musically from the pond. The shadows of beeches are blue in the winter twilight and there are windbreaks of evergreens placed behind the benches where nurses sit comfortably in the sunshine and watch children making snow men. Snow gives an air of fantasy to the monument that celebrates the first use of ether in surgery. (We were brought up on the theory that the group of statues showed the first patient being etherized —and not enjoying it much—and we suffered an intellectual shock when we were informed lately that we were looking at the Good Samaritan at work. We still prefer our interpretation to the official one.) Snow makes the glass and the polished doorknobs and knockers along the Beacon Street side of the Garden shine with particular brightness. It makes the statue of Edward Everett Hale seem taller than ever and frosts his beard so that he looks the way he did when he used to come to school to talk to us.

He would always begin: "I suppose I ought to call you 'young ladies' but when I asked a group of you here once whether that was the right way to address you, you all began at once 'Callusgirls! Callusgirls! Callusgirls!' So I shall call you 'girls.' "

After that he would tell us how, when he was a small boy, he lived in a very busy household and never seemed to have any time to himself until one day he went up into the attic and found an old box, a sea chest perhaps, painted blue. He pulled it out from under the eaves and dragged it over to a window and sat down on its faded blue lid. Over the tops of trees, he could see the curve of a river shining beyond a green field and hummingbirds coming in and out of a trumpet vine and the flash of scythes, as the long grass fell in windrows, and two horses standing beside each other in quiet friendship.

He would put his chin on the window sill and think—not about anything special—he would just think. Everybody, he said, ought to have a blue box for thinking. Then he used to recite his simple rule for a good life; "Look upward, not down. Look outward, not in. Look forward, not back. Lend a hand."

He was a plain man, looking much like his statue, but we are glad to remember that he looked beautiful to us, even though we were laughed at for saying so. Benevolent was too large a word for us then, we suppose, and perhaps we were right anyway.

Even when the snow begins to melt and paths are muddy, it is hard to believe that the Garden was once open water and that the British launched the boats in which they set out for Concord from a beach not far from Arlington Street. Boys went swimming and boating and fishing, and played Robinson Crusoe and pirates and sunken treasure all through the islands and channels in the marsh of what is still called the Back Bay. Not only the Garden, as we know it, but all the land between it and the Harvard Medical School was filled in so that the city could grow westward. A thousand acres was added to the city in this way, at no cost at all. Indeed, the state made about three million dollars on the transaction for the contractors who hauled the dirt from Needham were paid in building lots. Some lots were assigned to the state and sold. The money received was given to Harvard University, to Tufts College, and to other Massachusetts institutions.

A young Englishman, who came to the city at the time the Back Bay was being filled in, told us of lying awake in his room on Charles Street on hot nights and hearing, long before dawn, the two-wheeled dump carts that carried the dirt begin to rumble across the city. The gravel was brought on trains that ran all night. He could hear the sound of the trains in the distance, then the creaking roll of the carts, the slow pounding of horses' feet, the thump and slither as the gravel was dumped, then men shouting at their horses, the grating noise of shovels on gravel, and at last the empty carts rattling off again.

The filling in of the Back Bay would have been a great task with bulldozers and tractors; with two-wheeled carts and hand shovels it was an extraordinary achievement. The place from which the dirt was brought, near Kendrick's Bridge in Needham, is still like a desolate canyon where erosion has been at work for ages and it is hard to believe, especially when spring comes to the Garden, that there is any connection between the two places. The Garden is full of color from the time the willows around the pond first turn golden. A warm day comes, the willows are like green rain, beech leaves are bronze, magnolias bloom pink and ivory. For a time the board walks are left down. Children's running feet echo on them and where they jump off to the paths, footprints fill with water.

Then, as suddenly as the snow came, the grass is greener than grass ever was and tulips are in full bloom—pink, scarlet, white, crimson, yellow—with pansies half hidden by the jade-green twisted leaves above them. The Garden is full of photographers carrying cameras loaded with color film and patiently trying to catch the translucence of sunlit tulip petals. Not long after dawn there are men and women watching birds through binoculars because, oddly enough, with the city sleeping around it, the Garden is one of the best places to see certain birds on migration. Like Bostonians, birds are conservative. They prefer places they have always known; apparently there is something unchanging and familiar about the Garden that gives them a sense of security. The people who stroll contentedly in the Garden feel somewhat as the birds do. Even those who prefer tulips planted casually in a border find something satisfying in the stiff familiar rows, in the knowledge that no pink tulip will ever create a scandal by straying into a bed of white ones, in the assurance that with inhuman perfection all will bud and grow, open and fade in perfect harmony. It was strange to see jonquils and narcissus in these beds during the war, as strange as the procession of figures in khaki and blue on the bridge and the hideous brown paint on the dome of the State House. For many of us the war was not officially over until the oblong beds glowed with tulips again. Bostonians take such pride in the tulips that although thousands of people come to see them, we have never seen a petal touched. Their very perfection protects them.

In summer there is an almost tropical feeling about the Garden. Palms appear near the gates. Fuchsias and ivy and begonias and coleus—all the bedding plants the Victorians cherished—are crammed into the flower beds. The scent of sun-warmed heliotrope greets the visitor soon after he leaves the gasoline-laden air of the street and enters the Garden. Fountains throw diamonds and pearls of coolness into the sunshine. There is thick shade under the beeches. Willow branches move in the light breeze that ripples the water around the swan boats. The swan boats are out with their benches shining with scarlet paint and the swans at the sterns gleaming white. Summer is not over until they have gone wherever it is that swan boats go for the winter.

Our grandmother used to take us to ride on them. We did not feel the full dignity of grandmotherhood until we gave our granddaughter her first ten cents' worth of swan-boating. In a changing world, swan boats remain the same. There are few places on this planet where you can be sure of seeing perfectly happy people, but a swan boat is one. If we were escaping from the police, we would hide in plain sight

29. BOSTON, MASSACHUSETTS. It is not really spring until the swan boats are out in the Public Garden.

on a swan boat where we are certain no one ever hid before:
swan boats are for innocent hearts only.

We knew a bride, who was a happy wife for more than
thirty years. She spent her wedding morning with all her
bridesmaids riding on the swan boats. She always claimed
that it was the only way to get ready for a wedding. Perhaps
there are other ways as good but we are inclined to agree
with her. A bride, in tulip time, might well dismiss her boat
with Lohengrin's words:

Nun sei gedankt, mein lieber Schwan.

Yes, on the whole, the Garden has a unique place among
village greens.

30. PLYMOUTH, MASSACHUSETTS. This green was the training ground of the oldest permanent settlement in New England.

CHAPTER 9

Greens by the Sea

*A*s we go south from Boston we are increasingly conscious of the sea. Superficially a village green near the sea looks much like one inland. The grass is there and the sunlight spattering through moving elm leaves. The white houses and the church spire are not very different from those of a common set among hills. It is small things that tell us the sea is near: the smell of drying fish blowing past the meetinghouse, paths of crushed oyster shells leading away from the green, an arch made from the jaw of a whale harpooned a century ago, gardens edged with scallop shells. Perhaps some child has left a horseshoe crab on a doorstep· or you see on a porch an octagonal seat of blue and white porcelain brought long ago from Canton in a clipper ship.

We feel somehow that the quiet green triangle on which we walk is only the beginning of a path that leads round Cape Horn to the Orient. In the square white houses facing the greens, oriental rugs and lacquer screens and paintings on silk seem at home. They have always been there and still belong. It is the carved chests from Italy and tapestries from France that look foreign.

The sea often leaves a town with no central green at all. If it began as a fishing village, a town continues to look towards the water that first brought it life. Its streets run back from the wharves and along the shore. Its focus is still the harbor and its green is sea green—with white sails upon it.

Yet even in seaside villages we find evidence of the idea of land owned in common. Plymouth, the oldest permanent settlement in New England, was established on the principle of communism. The system was discarded because it proved unproductive, but many Plymouth landmarks were built on what·was once common land and the first houses were started as common property but completed by individual owners. There was a Common House—a tablet opposite the end of Carver Street shows where it stood. Miles Standish was chosen captain by popular vote: an early instance of American democracy in action. On Burial Hill at the head of Town Square are the sites of a watch tower and an old fort, evidence of common effort for protection. The statue of Massasoit, friend of the Pilgrims, looks down from Cole's Hill, which was common ground in a grim and terrible sense, for those who died that first winter were buried there and corn planted over the graves so that the Indians would not know how many there were.

At a great dinner, given to mark the two hundred and fiftieth anniversary of the founding of Plymouth, the guests found on their plates for the first course five kernels of parched corn. This was the ration for one day in the year 1623. When we consider such hardships as this, when we climb Burial Hill and puzzle out the Latin inscription on Governor Bradford's gravestone, it seems more than ever important that we should not "basely relinquish what the fathers with difficulty obtained."

There are interesting commons in many towns between Boston and Plymouth. Near Bridgewater Common stands the Washburn House, built in 1700, a two-and-a-half-story building, its gables weathered by the same storms that bent the old trees bordering the walk. It must already have looked old when it was confiscated from its Tory owner in the Revolution.

At West Bridgewater, the green is unusual in being near the Town River, for rivers, like the sea, tend to push commons farther inland and cause a town to develop along a main street. Besides the common, the town has another unusual space for recreation in Memorial Park, which is centered around the site of an old grist mill. The stream, which once kept the big stones turning, now travels through a chain of ornamental falls so that the place is filled with the sound of rushing water.

The land on which West Bridgewater has grown up was purchased from Massasoit for thirty dollars' worth of merchandise, including coats, hoes, hatchets, and knives. The deed is still in the possession of the Bridgewater Historical Society.

In this same region is Hanover Center with a pleasant green on which stands the Samuel Stetson House. This handsome place, built in 1694, is now owned by the Society for the Preservation of New England Antiquities and is open to the public. Duxbury, just beyond, is another old settlement which set aside common land for the pasturage of cattle. Indeed Miles Standish and John Alden went there because they needed space for their increasing herds. Both men rest in the Old Burying Ground at Hall's Corner, but the exact location of Alden's grave is not certain. On one marker in this graveyard the stonecutter has engraved a woman's name and then has added with candor, and perhaps a certain amount of kindness, "The chisel can't help her any."

There is no green in all this region that seems so beautiful to us as the one at Cohasset. Although it started as a fishing village—the place was discovered by Captain John Smith in 1614 and was dependent on fishing for many years —Cohasset's spacious green lies within sight and sound of the sea. In the fall, when we passed this common, the elms were dropping gilded leaves into a pool as quiet as an inland lake, yet the tide was rushing up into a rocky cove near by, the church bells were ringing, the bell buoys were answering them out of a wall of fog offshore.

There are fifty-one bells in the carillon in the Gothic tower of the Episcopal Church. We climbed it once and saw, as well as heard, the bells ring out *For those in peril on the sea.* We wondered where the breeze carried the tune. The thought that ships outside in the fog may hear it is part of life on the green, as is Minot's Light flashing its bright and constant warning through the darkness.

Cohasset Common is beautiful at any time of year—in its autumn green and gold, in the winter when the meetinghouse spire is white against a stormy sky, in spring when the first green mist clouds the elms. There is always a quiet charm about the pond, the tall flagpole reaching up among the trees, and the white buildings around the green. Perhaps the loveliest time to see all this part of Massachusetts is when the climbing roses are in bloom. The salt breezes and the fog seem to bring a special brilliance to Paul's Scarlets, a special delicacy and freshness to Silver Moons and Van Fleets. They take possession of white fences or gray rocks or weathered shingles all the way to the Cape and out beyond to the Vineyard and Nantucket.

Yet as you cross the canal and reach Cape Cod, you are in a world subtly different from the one you have just left. Here the wind blows all day long and twists the pines so that they seem to belong on some old cabinet of Chinese lacquer. It makes houses hug the ground for comfort and keeps kites in the air all day and sets the sails of windmills creaking. With the scent of roses and of the sea, it mingles bayberry and the hot, smoky, ecstatic fragrance of a clambake on the beach.

Neither the wind nor the sea, from which it blows, nor sandy soil are materials from which village greens are naturally made, and yet one of the most interesting of Massachusetts commons is at Falmouth. Here around a wide-fenced green are old houses that witnessed the attack of the British in the Revolution. They returned to attack it again in the War of 1812, but this time the watchers on the captains' walks above the square houses could have seen a

31. COHASSET, MASSACHUSETTS. Here is peace and unchanging beauty in a green by the sea.

[*149*]

British ship captured. Paul Revere is connected with Falmouth Green, for in the steeple of the church that faces it hangs a bell which he cast. Like the others he made for New England churches it carries the inscription:

The living to the church I call:
Unto the grave I summon all.

Some of those summoned would have had to return across far oceans. With good reason, the railed walks on the roofs were sometimes called widows' walks. Women through the years watched from those walks for many a ship that never returned.

More cheerful thoughts are suggested by the term, captain's walk. Sometimes the watcher was a man who had in his time made the voyage round the Horn, bought sea otter skins on the northwest coast of America, and traded them in China for tea and ginger in blue and white jars and for painted porcelain, but now, retired, he still followed his ships half across the globe in his mind's eye and watched through his spyglass for the flutter of his own house flag.

With what pleasure he would come down from the roof and say to his wife, "I have sighted the Sea Gull. I shall bring Captain Howe back to dinner, my dear. I hope we have something good . . . salt fish!!! Jerusha, not fish—And salt at that! Kill a chicken, kill a pig, send out for an elephant or a peacock—anything but fish!" Whereupon he would pull on his bright, brass-buttoned, blue coat, straighten his wig, set his hat slightly over one eye, and stroll down to the wharf, pretending to be in no hurry.

Girls and boys—and wives and mothers and sisters, too—would be all excitement when the captain's own chests were carried up from the wharf and the presents for them and the neighbors were unpacked. There would be carved red and white, slanting-eyed chessmen standing on bases made of three balls one inside the other, black lacquer boxes, teapots in padded straw baskets, bronze gongs, chests of tea. Almost certainly there would be shawls from India, Cashmere

32. FALMOUTH, MASSACHUSETTS. Across this green retired sea captains often watched for their returning vessels.

shawls, woven on small hand looms and put together so cleverly they appeared made of one piece. For the captain's daughter there might be a burnoose of scarlet or peacock blue with a border of heavy white silk embroidery. To wear with it would be jewelry of tortoise shell covered with a delicate tracery of gold with pearls and turquoises among the fragile leaves and flowers. Curious weapons—swords, daggers, guns—would fascinate the boys. There was never any trouble finding cabin boys on a green near the sea.

Thirty miles out to sea, beyond the Cape, the tradition of land owned in common was followed by the first settlers of Nantucket Island. Here wide expanses of moorland, still known as the Commons, were once used for pasturing sheep. Now the air sweeps over prickly shining holly and bends scrub oaks and pines and cedars. There are masses of purple heather and bayberry and wild flowers of many kinds. Sunset over the Commons when land as well as sea catches and holds the tints of the sky is a sight to be remembered.

In contrast to the wind-swept natural beauty of the Commons is the man-made charm of Nantucket town. Here the commonly owned central space—called Town Square—is no longer a green expanse but a stretch of lumpy cobblestones. Somehow the effect is attractive though the cobbles certainly present a hazard to the riders of tandem bicycles, a favorite form of locomotion in Nantucket.

Here again, as at Falmouth or Old Lyme, the Orient seems near. True, the Atlantic washes the shores of Nantucket, but the bank is the Pacific Bank and the former Custom House is now the Pacific Club. The original members of this club were descendants of men who had sailed whaling ships into the Pacific Ocean.

An antique shop on any common near the sea has a different flavor from one near an inland green. Instead of oxbows there are figureheads of ships and weather vanes carry dolphins instead of cows. The presence of the sea makes a Nanking chocolate pot look as much at home as a Bennington pie plate does in Vermont. Nantucket's antiques

33. Nantucket, Massachusetts. Town Square, once a green but now a stretch of cobblestones, remains the center of the town.

are even more specialized. Not merely ships, but whaling ships, are responsible for the jagging wheels, the scrimshaw work, the whale oil lamps, which the visitor soon comes to consider as proper to the place as carved butter molds to dairy country.

Whaling is the obvious influence in Nantucket's past. Less often mentioned is the fact that many of the early settlers were Quakers. The Indians called the island Canopache, the Place of Peace. The name still seems appropriate: there is a serene Quakerlike charm about the little gray houses. These simple dwellings on curving cobblestoned lanes are a contrast to the stately mansions which front Main Street just off Town Square. Their pillared porticoes suggest the elegance of the great houses of the Louisiana or Virginia plantations.

However, when Nantucket sea captains settled down, they wanted no more of the wide open spaces but were content to live close enough to their neighbors to know who was having fish balls for breakfast. Perhaps the Starbuck mansions are the handsomest of their houses but there are many others to see within easy range of Town Square. From the Square we easily make the transition from bicycle to whaleboat with a visit to the Whaling Museum, where harpoons and ship models make very real Captain Ahab's chase of the white whale. Not far away at the Maria Mitchell House, the birthplace of the astronomer, we have the feeling that with Nantucket as a starting point, we touch not only the world but the universe. We touch it in a different way in the Friends' Meetinghouse. There bare floors and hard benches in a room lighted only by candles make us aware of how right is the name, Canopache for the place where we stand as well as for the island itself.

The word keeps echoing through our minds. Even when Town Square is busiest, there is an air of quiet friendliness about it. It stays serene in spite of summer visitors and accepts them and their bicycles as calmly as it used to welcome men home from the sea. We have an impression that the island is always more than just what we see before us. It is small but seems spacious. It is away from the world yet touches a wider horizon than many a large seaport. It is forthright and busy, yet has the quality of a dream.

Standing in Town Square and breathing the sea-softened air, we realize wistfully and perhaps enviously, too, that on Nantucket Island it is only right and proper that the inhabitants of the world should be divided into two classes—Islanders and Off-Islanders—and that we started four or five generations too late ever to be an Islander.

At Martha's Vineyard—"another island" according to the tourists' folder on Nantucket—we discovered a green which had developed in an unusual way. For more than a century there have been summer camp meetings at Oak Bluffs and the town has grown up around the tabernacle in Trinity Park, just as other towns have grown around a white meetinghouse on a village green. Oak Bluffs, however, began not as a collection of log cabins in the wilderness but as a city of tents in an oak grove. Even the tabernacle itself was once made of canvas. The first tents were set up in a circle and later the town planners never laid out a road in a straight line. Real estate developments in turn had loops, circles, ovals, and hairpin curves.

Here and there were open spaces called parks and in the long drawn out law suit over these parks, there is a reflection of the New England attitude toward common land. The owners of the developments had never formally surrendered their rights in the parks either to the owners of the houses around them or to the town. After many years, the men who had started the enterprise sold all the land they still owned, including the parks, to a speculator who planned to cut them up and sell them as building lots. The case was finally carried to the Supreme Court of the Commonwealth and it was the younger Oliver Wendell Holmes who wrote the opinion that kept the parks for public use. The principle, which was first stated by him, was upheld through a second law suit. The verdict was that the parks were "dedicated" to the public use and that the acceptance of such dedication need not be formally made by the town. The acceptance was made by the public in its customary use of the land. In a section of the country where the central common is so much a part of the life of a town, this seems a just and natural decision. Whether at that time it would have been made outside New England can be only a matter for speculation.

Oak Bluffs is no longer a city of tents but of tiny wooden cottages which suggest that tents were their forerunners. On the curving roads around the tabernacle the cottages stand on pieces of ground not much larger than good-sized rugs. Built in the age of the jig saw, in the style called Gothic, they follow a basic pattern. There is a pointed gable in front, a porch below it, and upstairs little fret-sawed balconies under each window. Around the eaves appears more jig-saw work, reminding us of the Hamburg edging that used to be sewn on petticoat ruffles of the same period as the houses. Much love and art have been expended upon the painting of the cottages with rather remarkable results —yellow houses with green lace edging, pink with white, pale blue with crimson, terra cotta and turquoise. The color schemes suggest the costumes of the seventies, the period when many of the houses were built. In his delightful book, *Martha's Vineyard: Summer Resort,* Henry Beetle Hough quotes a description of one of the parlors: "The ceiling is of robin's egg blue, the panels in the wall are of terra cotta and light olive; the frame work in Indian red with a border of salmon shade surrounding the ceiling, with cornice of Pompeian red bordered with gilt."

With such a background, it is not surprising that women were always referred to as elegant females and it is pleasant to imagine them in long draped skirts playing croquet with whiskered gentlemen in candy-striped blazers. We can picture charming evenings when the cottages were hung with Japanese lanterns, when colored light glowed softly on flowers, moss, shells, balconies, banners, and scrollwork and was at times dimmed by blazing rockets dripping golden rain.

It is a long way from the austerity of meetinghouses and Puritan gloom to the Methodist Tabernacle in Trinity Park. Although the tabernacle has drawn its strength from people in gay summertime mood, it has both dignity and power. It stands in a spacious circular greensward from which radiate irregular walks. The tabernacle is twenty-four sided, open to the air, with seats arranged circularly about the pulpit. Light comes in from above through the clerestory, above which is a square tower and resting on this a hexagonal lantern. Flower beds brighten the park and fine old oaks, sometimes bent and broken by storms, recall those first days of worship in the grove.

The arrangement of the roads around the tabernacle is as dizzying as the Gothic rainbow of the cottages. We felt as we did when we were lost in Hampton Court Maze. There was a little cottage painted yellow with an edging of what looked like red tatting which we kept finding every time we thought we were going to escape. At one time we decided that the simplest solution would be to buy it and spend the summer, but by sheer accident we found our way, took the boat back to the continent, and went on to Rhode Island.

White sails on blue water, clambakes on sandy beaches, lighthouses flashing at night, sea gulls dipping and veering, all let us know that this state is well named. Indeed it took its name from the island on which Newport stands.

The colony's charter obtained from Charles the Second states, "that no person within the said colony shall be anywise molested, punished, disquieted, or called into question for any differences in matters of religion, but that every person may at all times hereafter freely and fully enjoy his own conscience in matters of religious concernments." This was not the spirit to develop a tight little community on a green around one meetinghouse with all the good people inside and all the others out. On this account, and also because the people turned their eyes seaward, village greens are rarely seen in Rhode Island.

34. NEWPORT, RHODE ISLAND. In Touro Park, William Ellery Channing, a great liberal, presides over a green expanse.

More typical is a place like Touro Park in Newport. This park may well stand for the development of a community with a heritage of religious liberalism: It was given to Newport by Judah Touro, son of the first regular rabbi of Temple Israel, which is probably the oldest synagogue in America. At his death, Touro left large sums of money to churches of many faiths.

In Touro Park the statue of William Ellery Channing recalls another liberal of Rhode Island. He was born in Newport but much of his work as a leader of Unitarian thought was done in Massachusetts. It seems appropriate that the voice which shook the foundations of Puritanism should come from Rhode Island. Roger Williams carried liberal thought away from Massachusetts; Channing brought it back. Through him the astounding idea that people could be good and happy at the same time began to be entertained in houses around the village greens. Channing, as much as any one man, was responsible for the final separation in 1833 of church and state in Massachusetts. In preaching that "we must start religion in our own souls" and that "the human mind can most mournfully misrepresent the deity," Channing helped to change more than one of the Puritan meetinghouses in Massachusetts to "The First Church, Unitarian."

Near his statue in Touro Park is the Old Stone Mill, a landmark once thought to be a tower built by Norsemen. Longfellow connected it with a skeleton found near Fall River. In "The Skeleton in Armor" he has the dead Viking say:

> *Far in the Northern Land,*
> *By the wild Baltic's strand*
> *I, with my childish hand*
> *Tamed the gerfalcon;*
> *And, with my skates fast-bound,*
> *Skimmed the half-frozen Sound,*
> *That the poor trembling hound*
> *Trembled to walk on.*

The Viking grows to manhood, becomes a marauder of the seas, carries off the daughter of a prince, sails westward with her, and

There for my lady's bower
Built I the lofty tower,
Which, to this very hour,
Stands looking seaward.

The skeleton, according to modern opinion, was probably that of an Indian and the tower was a windmill built in the late seventeenth century by Governor Benedict Arnold, father of General Benedict Arnold.

Half a century before the mill was built, in 1636, Roger Williams paddled a canoe down the Seekonk River and received a greeting from an Indian who was standing on a rock on the riverbank. "What cheer, Netop?" the Indian said.

This salutation pleased Williams. He understood that "Netop" meant friend. Not far away where three hills rose out of the river land and where there was a spring of clear water, he placed his new town.

"Having a sense of God's merciful providence unto me I called this place Providence," Williams wrote. "I desired it might be for a shelter for persons distressed for conscience."

Providence, though now a large and busy city, still offers peaceful areas of green. One of the pleasantest is in front of the First Baptist Meetinghouse, a church famous in New England, surrounded by trees and green grass, with a background that suggests a village rather than a city. The spire is another reminiscent of those designed by Christopher Wren. The transition from square through octagonal shapes to a point is adroitly and beautifully managed. The bell is appropriately inscribed:

For freedom of conscience the town was first planted.
Persuasion, not force was used by the people:
This church is the eldest and has not recanted,
Enjoying and granting bell, temple, and steeple.

35. PROVIDENCE, RHODE ISLAND.   The world is pleasanter when cities are
not entirely paved with concrete.

The Mall in Exchange Place is another restful green place. This oasis of grass and trees in the center of Providence is convincing proof that the world is a far pleasanter place when cities are not all paved with concrete. Like greens in quieter places, this one seems an appropriate spot for soldiers' monuments.

Providence has always been famous for hospitality. Long before it was possible to look down on Exchange Place from tall office buildings, there was a tradition of delicious food generously served in handsome rooms from beautiful glass and china and silver. We can get a very good idea of eighteenth-century entertainments in this and other seaport cities by visiting the Colonial House, which is connected with the Museum of the Rhode Island School of Design. Here are rooms furnished with some of the finest mahogany pieces ever made in America. Here are tall chocolate pots, great hospitable punch bowls, and delicate cups without handles brought from China. Against this background it is easy to imagine the originals of Copley or Stuart portraits in lace and brocade and powdered hair moving through candlelit rooms. We can see some delightfully pompous negro butler welcoming guests, hear the clink of a silver ladle against Waterford crystal or armorial porcelain, smell that cheering blend of tea and lemon and rum.

In Providence and Boston, Portsmouth and Wiscasset, Salem, Nantucket, and Newburyport, the salt breeze that blew through mall or square, green or common brought with it something cosmopolitan to those who lived in the tall houses with the classic porches and moved through parlors that smelled of sandalwood and spiced rose leaves. It did not, however, blow away a certain homely quality. The people served old Madeira in Providence dining rooms, but they served Rhode Island jonnycake, too. How the corn should be ground and how it is turned from creamy ivory meal to what Thomas Hazard called ambrosia can be learned from his *Jonny Cake Papers,* which also reveal, in the "Last Baking," how his grandfather's incomparable cook, Phyllis, was the cause of the French Revolution!

Providence, along with the tradition of the only proper way to make johnnycake, has preserved a number of interesting buildings within walking distance of Exchange Place. In spite of its liberalism the city has had the New England spirit that makes people treasure old things—just because they are old. This is a conservative trait but we may well be grateful to the impulse that made people hold on to Lowestoft bowls and block-front secretaries at a time when it was the fashion to buy something newer, shinier—and uglier.

Landmarks like the Old State House with the green in front were indeed worth saving, worth looking at too, now that they have been saved. The Old State House is a long way architecturally from those first, dark, shaggy little houses with thatched roofs and oil-paper windows. In fact, it it almost unbelievable that only a little more than a century after the construction of these crude shelters, the most beautiful houses in America were being built. In some cases the architects are known, but in many more instances the houses were the work of able carpenters, who had in their pockets books of designs published in England, in their heads an idea of how such houses could be built—under conditions the designer knew nothing about—and in their hands the skill to do it. Tools were few and simple but guiding them were craftsmanship and experience. A master builder may have begun training at three when he went with his mother to a neighborhood barn-raising or to the building of a new meetinghouse on the common. From his earliest years he absorbed knowledge of materials and tools and worked with men who knew what they were doing. He learned by what is now termed the project method.

In travelling through Rhode Island and looking at the John Brown house or the Crawford Allen house in Providence, the Bradford house in Bristol, or at the carving over the door of St. John's Rectory in Newport, we must realize

that such beauty exists partly because a hundred years earlier men who pastured cattle on village commons had to build their houses with their own hands and with the help of their neighbors. We heard the other day of four ex-soldiers who were building their own houses together. Perhaps some of our present problems could be solved if we could summon again the old spirit of neighborly helpfulness.

Rhode Island and Massachusetts are friends now, we are glad to say; the quarrels about boundaries are over. Such were the difficulties, however, that a Massachusetts lawyer described Rhode Island as being bounded on the north by a bramble bush, on the west by a swarm of bees, on the south by a blue jay, and on the east by five hundred foxes with their tails on fire. As we walk up and down the hills of Providence and read the names of the streets—Benevolent, Peace, Benefit, Friendship—we are more likely to feel that Rhode Island is bounded by a state of mind. It is true, the rock from which the Indian hailed Roger Williams has disappeared—only a tablet marks the place now—but the greeting, "What cheer, Netop?" seems as friendly and welcoming to the visitor today as it did to that first settler long ago.

37. MIDDLEBURY, CONNECTICUT. Nowhere is there greater beauty and serenity than on this green.

CHAPTER *10*

The Lovely Greens of Connecticut

The harmony of trees, turf, and buildings seems complete and satisfying on the lovely greens in Connecticut, and the towns there have a wonderful air of well-being. Perhaps they struggled less for existence than other New England villages and in a kinder climate developed more easily. In spring, when the tobacco nets look like patches of distant snow, there is still real snow elsewhere in New England. In the fall, when the ski tow is already running on Mount Mansfield, the Connecticut hills have been only lightly touched by frost and the great golden tobacco leaves hang to dry in well-ventilated barns that look strange to eyes accustomed to the tightly clapboarded buildings of the country farther north. Perhaps the gentler climate made the original settlers less rigid in their outlook than the Puritans of Massachusetts or it may be that the milder ones migrated from Boston because the religion there was too harsh. However it happened, Connecticut greens with their surrounding buildings have a charm that sets them apart and they seem to us among the most beautiful in New England.

To the north, the majority of the greens are triangular, although many started out as rectangles, but before long two of the corners were reduced to make an angle where a main road split into two branches. It may be that ox teams began this process. Later stagecoaches and then buggies cut farther into the corners until automobiles made the final sharp point. Now it is forgotten that certain northern greens ever were anything but triangles neatly edged with concrete.

In Connecticut, a great many towns have shown sufficient force of character to keep their commons rectangular as at Meriden Green, once a training ground for soldiers of the Revolution. Monuments to soldiers of that war are less usual than those of the Civil War, but Meriden has one, appropriately placed on the green where they used to drill. There are also memorials to those who fought in other wars.

Branford's green, not far away, is a generous triangle, large enough to make an attractive center for the town's public buildings. Here are paths shaded by elm trees to make a pleasant place for strolling and comfortable benches for rest during the heat of a summer's day. Room has been saved too from the demands of traffic for a wide margin of grass around the Honor Roll.

In Branford, Trinity Episcopal Church with its Gothic window replaces the meetinghouse of an earlier day. When the old building was torn down, the farmers of the region, with characteristic Yankee inventiveness and economy, sawed up the ancient, fluted pillars to make well curbings, some of which exist today. Only the town hall and the courthouse still have their tall columns.

In the busy city of Waterbury to the north, the green is long and narrow and, in spite of its modern look, very old. Settlers came to Waterbury as early as 1674 and the town, clustering around the green, was incorporated two years later. The soil was so poor and the hills so rugged that the first scouts who came to examine the place reported that "our apprehensions are it may accommodate but thirty families."

38. BRANFORD, CONNECTICUT. This triangular green is still used and enjoyed.

Today Waterbury is a city of about one hundred thousand, relying, as have so many Connecticut towns, not on fertility of soil but of invention. Here brass was the material on which native ingenuity was expended. Indeed the workers of Waterbury may be said to have turned it to gold.

Many Connecticut greens are quiet places, safely shut away from the bustle of life, but Waterbury's open space under the elms is enjoyed by hundreds every day. It is still, as originally intended, common property for the benefit of all the people.

In contrast to the busy center at Waterbury is the quiet green of Middlebury. It is on a plateau and seems a century away from the industrial bustle of Connecticut. Named because it is halfway between Waterbury and Woodbury, the town has a green that invites the description, "elm-shaded." Nowhere is there a greater feeling of serenity than on this green smooth lawn under the great trees. Although the buildings surrounding it are not very old—the earlier Congregational Church and town hall were burned down some years ago and the present ones are restorations—they have the look of ageless beauty.

Middlebury is one of the few towns that still has a blacksmith shop near the green. Of course in the days of horse-drawn traffic a town could hardly exist without a smithy, which was always a magnet for children. They would gather round the forge, listen to the ringing of the anvil, and glory in the wonderful aroma of hot metal and scorched hoof and hair, while the smith hammered the horseshoe in place. There was almost always a blacksmith shop near where the stagecoaches changed horses. We can imagine how the coach sounded as it rolled up to the smithy when the leader had a loose shoe—the beat of hoofs on the soft dust, the jingle, the rattle, the blaring horn, the creak of leather. These sounds have ceased now but we can still hear the hammer and the anvil, if we go to Middlebury.

Today, blacksmiths visit their customers with a portable outfit. A farmer we know sent for the smith the other day.

"But he wanted eight dollars; can you beat that? Eight dollars for putting on one shoe? 'Why,' I said to him, 'I can get the best doctor in town to come out here for five dollars.' "

"Is that so," says he, "and can your doctor shoe a horse?"

A particularly beautiful Connecticut green is at Brooklyn. It is overlooked by handsome, eighteenth-century houses and the ell of the General Wolfe Tavern, once run by General Israel Putnam, stands near. An English traveller, who visited America some years after the Revolution, commented on the fact that so many inns were kept by former officers of Washington's army. He stated that at least one-third of the general officers had been innkeepers before they entered the army and apparently many returned to their earlier occupation.

It is doubtful, however, if any other officer had General Putnam's reason for taking up tavern keeping. His wife insisted that the expense of entertaining his many friends was ruining him and that he should keep a tavern so as to charge them for their food and drink. He did so but we hardly think his heart was in it. It is difficult to think of him as a smugly genial innkeeper for there was nothing placid about General Putnam. We see him leading his men into the water, wading out waist deep to return the British schooner's fire and send her crew scurrying to their boats, or at Bunker Hill relaying the order, "Don't fire till you see the whites of their eyes!" When he heard the news of the Concord fight, he left his plough in the field near Brooklyn Green and rushed off just as he was to join the army at Cambridge. It is at Brooklyn above his grave that his memorial stands, a bronze statue of him on horseback.

There is a characteristic story about Putnam and a wolf, which had been killing sheep not far from Abington. Putnam and five other men finally caught sight of her and followed her up a narrow ravine until she disappeared into a cave. At this point his companions had gone about as far as they cared to, but Putnam fastened a rope around his waist, grabbed his gun, and crawled right into the dark hole in the

39. EAST HADDAM, CONNECTICUT. The statue of Nathan Hale commemorates a man who regretted that he had but "one life to give" for his country.

rocks. "Pull me out, when I jerk the rope," he told his companions.

He had not gone far when fearful snarls and a strong jerk on the rope made them haul so hard that they pulled Putnam out, cut and bruised by the sharp rocks, and with his shirt ripped off. But he crawled back again, fired his gun, and was at last dragged out choked and blinded by smoke, blackened, scraped raw, bleeding, deafened, but with the wolf firmly grasped by the ears.

A Connecticut green at Monument Hill in Coventry is associated with another hero, Nathan Hale, who was born in a house near that pleasant place and prepared for Yale in the minister's house near by. Coventry was a training ground for soldiers of the French and Indian War, the Revolution, the War of 1812, and the Civil War. No doubt soldiers have marched there many times since.

The green at East Haddam is also reminiscent of Hale and has on it a fine monument to him. After he left Yale, he taught school for two years in East Haddam, in a red schoolhouse that overlooked the river and the graveyard. Early in the Revolution, Hale enlisted in the Connecticut regiment. He served in the siege of Boston and in 1776 was made a captain. Later he was one of a daring group who captured a British provision-ship almost under the guns of a man-of-war.

Then he became a schoolteacher again but only as a disguise, and perhaps not a very good one. He could not entirely conceal the daring soldier under the appearance and speech of a Dutch schoolmaster, so he was captured in British territory while trying to get information about the enemy. The next day he was hanged as a spy.

Nathan Hale is a hero remembered not just for his patriotism but for his affirmation of it. "I regret that I have only one life to give for my country," set a pattern for other Americans who had only the silent kind of courage. Indeed, this heroic statement in the face of death may have helped the cause more than any military secrets he could have discovered.

The bust of Hale surmounting the column on the green represents him as a handsome young man with a fine shock of curly hair and a well-cut nose and mouth. This is the right face for a hero—earnest, bold, with lips that could speak eloquently, eyes to look danger squarely in the face.

Hale's old-fashioned river town of East Haddam is a restful place to be on a Sunday morning when the tones of a bell that once hung in a Spanish monastery ring out over the quiet green. The monastery was destroyed in the Napoleonic wars and the bell—it was cast in 815 A.D.—was brought to East Haddam, then a busy fishing and shipping center. Surely this bell from Spain must be the oldest in any meetinghouse on an American village green.

The tones of old bells are not the only sounds that have been heard through the centuries by those who live near meetinghouses. The seasons bring the same succession of sound today as they did when men trained on the greens for Washington's armies. Song sparrows sing, a little rustily perhaps, while there is still snow on the common. Young peepers call on cool April evenings. In late May the wind blows through full-grown leaves with a silky rustle. Then scythes ring against whetstones and, when clouds are high in the sky, bees zing straight through the air to a hollow tree. Now comes the hot dry whine of the locust till our ears crack with the rasping and the hot dry silence after it. Off in a tower of cloud there is thunder and rain splashes suddenly against the spire of the meetinghouse. Autumn makes blowing leaves rustle crisply overhead and underfoot, too, and crickets chirp slowly on frosty nights. The first snow falls and the silence is so deep that northern lights seem to crackle across it. These sounds remain.

Other sounds have changed. Once the every-day noises consisted of the tinkle of cowbells and sleigh bells, the clip-clop of horses' feet, the whirr of the scissor-grinder's wheel, the voices of men urging their oxen. It took forty yoke of

40. SOUTH WOODSTOCK, CONNECTICUT. Grass grows to hay here beneath elms planted to celebrate the Battle of Lexington.

oxen to haul the tall pines that made masts for the king's ships. Indoors, spinning wheels hummed and looms clacked. Sometimes the spinner would stop her wheel because she heard the howl of a wolf or an Indian war whoop echoing from the hemlocks on the hills through the elms of the village green. Was one reason for planting elms that, unlike evergreens, they made poor lurking places for Indians and wild animals? Possibly, but more likely, they were reminiscent of English elms and seemed dear and familiar to the first settlers, for they planted them at a time when cutting down trees was a more usual occupation than setting them out.

On the green at South Woodstock there are elms which were set out just after the Battle of Lexington. The news of what had happened on Lexington Green travelled fast and was celebrated in many ways. In far-off Kentucky woodsmen named their camp for the Massachusetts town and the elms in Woodstock were not the only ones planted in honor of the day. Grass is still allowed to grow into hay under the Woodstock elms and is cut with the scythe. Greens so treated do not have the velvet-smooth texture of the turf at Lexington or Middlebury, but it is surprising how green they look a few days after the hay is carried away. There are all kinds of textures in the grass of the greens. Some are shaggy and rough. Others are smooth but, for good reason, are worn bare in spots.

We rather like to see those worn places on the greens at Sturbridge and Craftsbury Common. They show that a green is in use and not just on exhibition. Perfect grass and happy children cannot grow on the same green. On the whole, we prefer children. Football, baseball, country dancing, croquet, and a fascinating game played by scaling the cover of a tin cracker box through the air—each leaves its characteristic pattern on grass once crossed by curving cow paths or worn by the feet of marching men.

In the old days the game that travelers often watched while they waited for the stage to change horses was bowling on the green. At South Woodstock the green must look much as it did when stagecoaches stopped at the Arnold Inn and, though the coaches look gay and fascinating in old prints, travel in them was not precisely luxurious. One traveler writes that:

The carriages were old and shackling and much of the harness was made of rope. One pair of horses carried the stage eighteen miles. We generally reached our resting place for the night, if no accident intervened, at ten o'clock and after a frugal supper, we went to bed with a notice that we should be called at three in the morning, which generally proved to be half past two. Then, whether it snowed or rained, the traveller must rise and make ready by the help of a horn lantern and a farthing candle, and proceed on his way over bad roads.

It took a week to get from Boston to New York by what the owner of one line of coaches advertised as "the most convenient and expeditious way of travelling that can possibly be had in America."

When railroads took the place of stagecoaches, inns like the Arnold Tavern at South Woodstock and the Bowen Tavern at Woodstock Hill were left without customers. The Bowen Tavern stands on a peaceful and pleasant green which, like other unspoiled ones, are usually to be found in small towns. It is possible, however, for a small town to develop into a large city and still retain the early spirit and the beauty of its green. Perhaps the most interesting example of progress without loss of charm is at New Haven where the first settlement took place in 1638. Soon afterwards the common was laid out and turned over to a Proprietors' Committee, which has administered it ever since. Much of the land around New Haven was originally so swampy that the Indians are said to have cut sticks for their arrows from the alders there. They sold their rights in New Haven and in a large tract of country occupied by other towns for twenty-three coats and a "particular coat" for the sachem, twelve spoons, twenty-four knives, twelve hatchets, and a number of hoes, porringers, and scissors.

The New Haven colony was laid out in nine squares, the

central one being the green. In the daytime, this was used for a market and at night, for the safekeeping and pasture of cattle. The first elms on the green were planted in 1686 when the people of the church met to bring furnishings for the house of their minister. One man, who had nothing else to give, brought two young elms and planted them at the door of the house. It continued to be the custom to plant elms around the green and many were set out in 1787. The gift to the minister proved to be a pleasure to many generations who have walked in the shade of New Haven's famous elms.

Very early in the history of the town, the green became a civic center. The first meetinghouse was built in 1639. Watchhouse, schoolhouse, jail, stocks, and whipping post soon followed. The whipping post was promptly put into use; one elder of the church publicly flogged his daughter there for going to a housewarming in a young man's company. The State House and County Court House were added in the early years of the eighteenth century but none of these older buildings is now standing.

The three churches we see on the green today were built between 1812 and 1815. The Center Congregational Church was designed by Ithiel Town. Trinity Episcopal Church next to it is also his work. This is one of the earliest churches to show the revival of Gothic feeling in church architecture in America. On the other side of Center Church is the United Church, planned by David Hoadley who also designed some of the most beautiful of the Connecticut churches, among them those at Avon and Milford. The Milford church was widely copied; Cheshire, Southington, and Litchfield, all used it as a model. Churches at Killingworth and Woodbury also show the influence of David Hoadley's designs.

In Connecticut, as in Massachusetts, church and state were closely related. The Congregational churches of Connecticut are a beautiful heritage from this period of spiritual and political unity, as are the village greens on which they

41. NEW HAVEN, CONNECTICUT. This green has been a civic and religious center since 1638.

stand. And nowhere is the value of common land more clearly shown than on New Haven Green, which is the starting point for the main streets of the city, a busy municipal, religious, and educational center, and yet a peaceful and pleasant resting place. The Proprietors' Committee has, indeed, fulfilled its obligations in the wise administration of the common land of New Haven.

CHAPTER *II*

Greens in the Mountains and Temple Hills

*L*ong after the towns of the New England seaboard were comfortably established around their village commons, the hills west and north, were still frontier country. Hunters, lumbermen, trappers, garrison men for Fort Dummer near Brattleboro, Vermont and for Fort No. 4 at Charlestown, New Hampshire, French and Indians on the warpath—all were scouting the woods of the North Country at a time when, on Boston Common, men and women strolled in the twilight dressed in silk, brocade, velvet, and lace. Charlestown's little group of six log houses inside a log fort was not built until 1744 and Fort Dummer, the farthest outpost of its time, but twenty years earlier.

Both the French in Canada and the colonial governments in New England offered bounties for scalps and the earliest roads in the hill country were travelled by scalping parties. In Massachusetts as much as a hundred pounds was offered for Indian scalps. Neither side was guiltless in this matter but the burden of revenge fell upon innocent women and children carried off from towns like Durham, New Hampshire, and Lancaster, Massachusetts. A few of these captives returned—one of our ancestors did so—but many of them never saw their homes again.

Stories of encounters with the Indians are part of the history of many towns now quiet settlements around green commons. Even places as near Boston as Framingham were on the frontier. When the road was first extended to Framingham it was thought that "men would never penetrate further westward into the wilderness." It would be difficult for those who lived through the French and Indian War there to recognize the peaceful common at Framingham Center. It is difficult for us to realize, as we rest on a bench under brilliant trees on a warm autumn afternoon, that only a little way from this very spot Indians once skulked through trees like these on their way to burn and slay and carry off captives. The early settlers could not possibly have visualized their common as it is today with the church spire rising out of the trees and the grass smoothly rolled, nor can we feel, except in a dim and shadowy way, what their life was when these villages were lonely islands in the dark sea of primeval forest.

The Old Connecticut Path, an Indian trail before the English ever saw America, crosses another Framingham common, a small triangular green where the statue of a minuteman using his powder horn to load his musket is the memorial to soldiers of the Revolution. In the graveyard nearby is buried Peter Salem, a slave, who killed Major Pitcairn at the Battle of Bunker Hill.

All these old towns have stories showing how the Indians were feared and dreaded, but occasionally there is one showing that the fear could be on the other side. An old record describes an event that occurred near Chelmsford, Massachusetts:

About the 15th of August, Capt. Mosely with sixty men met a company, judged about three hundred Indians, in a plain place where few trees were, and on both sides preparations were making for a Battle; all being ready on both sides to fight, Captain Mosely plucked

42. FRAMINGHAM, MASSACHUSETTS. In the eighteenth century this common was on the frontier.

off his Periwig, and put it into his Breeches, because it should not hinder him in fighting. As soon as the Indians saw that, they fell a Howling and Yelling most hideously and said, 'Umh, Umh, me no staw herre fight Engis mon, Engis mon got two hed, Engis mon got two hed; if me cut off un hed, he got noder a put on beder as dis' with such words in broken English and away they all fled and could not be overtaken any more afterwards.

Chelmsford is on a busy road to the North Country but its common still affords the traveller restful moments of green shade. The Unitarian Church which faces the green is a white building with a clock and open belfry. It is about a century old and is the latest of four meetinghouses built there since 1644, when some of the parishioners of the Rev. John Fiske from Wenham followed him. Fiske made the town famous in its day by the publication of the "Chelmsford Catechism." Chelmsford children were required to learn it and evidently gave their copies hard use in the process, for only one copy is now known to exist.

One of the town's Revolutionary soldiers, Joseph Spalding, was famous around the village common for having fired the first shot at Bunker Hill. He not only fired the first shot but did it ahead of time. At the moment his enthusiasm was not applauded; in fact, General Putnam rushed over and struck Spalding for disobeying orders. He guessed he deserved it, Spalding used to admit, but ever since the fight at Concord Bridge he'd been wanting to get another shot at the regulars.

"The blow Old Put hit me made a hole in my hat and left a scar on my head," he used to add, not without a trace of pride.

Long after Spalding ceased to tell the story to the boys of Chelmsford, the hat was still there in the house where he lived until at last the house and all its contents were destroyed by fire.

As we gaze on the common of almost any old New England town, it is natural to feel that the only way for a town to grow up is around such a central green space; that the meetinghouse, the school, the general store, the tavern, the mansion houses of the prosperous belong as they are placed here and could be arranged in no other way. Actually this is an illusion. The main street, the four corners, the market place are all workable community patterns. In fact, more people could be housed on a Louisiana sugar plantation with its fifty-room house, its slave quarters, its buildings for guests and overseers, its storerooms, and workshops than around a New England village common in the eighteenth century. The difference is not one of efficiency but of mental attitude. The plantations, the great farms of the rich Pennsylvania country, the old Dutch houses of northern New York like stone fortresses all have an air of shutting out the world. Only on a New England village green where everybody's cows graze in everybody's front yard does it seem that the world is shut in.

Compact villages are less usual as we go farther into the hills and the pale blue of the horizon is edged with the darker blue of mountains. Perhaps because level stretches of ground are scarce, perhaps because the close tie between meetinghouse and town had begun to loosen, or men who hewed farms out of forests were less dependent upon each other for protection than were their seventeenth-century ancestors—whatever the reason, we find that villages are more often built along a main street or centered at a crossroads than grouped around a central green.

At Fitzwilliam, New Hampshire, however, the traditional fashion was followed and there is an air of serenity about the fenced-in common. To this part of the country, early settlers often came with household goods loaded on oxcarts. They followed a blazed trail, when they were fortunate enough to find one; when they were not, they made a new trail, blazing it for the next comers. The first settler of Fitzwilliam, Benjamin Bigelow, used his oxcart not only for transportation but to live in, until he built his cabin, and

43. FITZWILLIAM, NEW HAMPSHIRE. An oxcart was the first dwelling on this fenced-in common.

Fitzwilliam's first new citizen was born in the shelter of this oxcart.

Like most of the settlements of the period—the last half of the eighteenth century—Fitzwilliam changed suddenly from a frontier town of rough huts to one with houses far handsomer than almost anyone thinks of building today. Just ten years after the oxcart was returned to its normal uses, the General Reed House was built, in 1773, at the eastern end of the common. The great central chimney suggests generous fireplaces inside. Outside the pediment above the door, a well-balanced arrangement of windows, and quoined corners add dignity to the design. Later in date but also distinguished for its fine proportions is the Congregational Church. Ionic columns support the portico which is unusual for its pediment containing an oval window and a decoration of palm branches. The steeple is graceful, and supplies one more illustration of the transition from square to octagonal. First comes the four-sided clock tower with a balustrade and sharp pyramids for finials. Then the belfry, also balustraded, but with urns for finials. The urns are repeated above as finials for the balustrades of two octagonal lanterns and the whole series inevitably leads the eye up to spire and weather vane.

Near Fitzwilliam, and once part of it, is Troy, also built around a neatly fenced common. It is a question whether to drive to these greens in June when the woods are filled with pale pink, shining-leaved laurel or in late September when the maples have changed to flaming scarlet and apricot, crimson and pale gold. The hills and valleys are beautiful at both times—and indeed in all other months, too.

On the windswept hilltop at Rindge is a common with a meetinghouse that has been resisting blizzards and hurricanes since 1797. This church illustrates still another way of designing a steeple: the clock tower is above the belfry. The whole building has the straightforward sturdiness of the steeple and seems expressive of the character of the men who cut their way into the North Country. Rindge once had the distinction of a hyphenated name—Rowley-Canada because some of the first settlers came from the Massachusetts town of Rowley and had also taken part in the expedition to Canada in 1690.

Among the Temple Hills is one of the most attractive commons in this part of New Hampshire. More than one child has thought the line in "America," about "Thy woods and templed hills," referred to his own hills and even when he has grudgingly relinquished the idea, never hears the song without remembering these thickly wooded slopes. Temple itself is a drowsy hill village with a beautiful outlook from its common. From the memorial tablets we judge it sent more soldiers to the Revolution than to any later war. The Old Burying Ground is part of the common, though fenced away from it, and is dedicated to "the wives and mothers of 1776."

A road from Temple to Peterborough was cut through the woods by soldiers and called the Revolutionary Road. This region, usually a quiet one, has hundreds of visitors on one day of the year—the last Sunday in August—when a Public Song Service is held at the top of one of the Temple Hills. In winter, skiers follow the Wapack Trail through these hills and up to the top of Pack Monadnock from which there is a view from the Atlantic to the Green Mountains. We remember it best on a blue October day when the whole tumbled expanse blazed with orange and red, blending in the distance to royal purple, and when the snow on Grand Monadnock's crest was as white as the spires from hidden village greens.

Grand Monadnock, or more simply Monadnock, is the presiding spirit of all this country. People speak of it not as scenery or something to climb but as a well-loved friend.

"How is the Mountain looking today?" is a question often asked over the telephone by unfortunates who have no view.

The answer may be, "Rather pale today," or "Sullen, with its cloud cap on," or "Every stone is shining; it's a Mountain Day."

44. RINDGE, NEW HAMPSHIRE. A large white meetinghouse dominates
this windswept hill common.

[*189*]

Emerson saw it and wrote about it when,

From the fixed cone the cloud-rack flowed
Like ample banner flung abroad
Round about a hundred miles . . .

He called it a "haughty hill" or an "airy fortress" and said, *The Titan minds his sky affairs.* He spoke of the people of the region as,

. . . men of bone and good at need
Rallying round a parish steeple.

He evidently knew Monadnock's majestic profile well, but his poem suggests the veneration in which the mountain is held rather than the affection felt for it. Monadnock is a mountain that people take to their hearts. There are only a few heights that seem to arouse just this sort of feeling— Chocorua in New Hampshire is one and Couching Lion in Vermont, another. The whole mass of Mount Desert is mourned over—and loved—in its fire-scarred desolation. To all these hills, New Englanders lift up their eyes for strength, and the steeples of the meetinghouses never seem to link earth and sky so definitely as in country where they reach towards some cloud-shadowed, rocky peak.

One of our favorite greens in this region is at Hancock, a quiet, unspoiled town with such an air of permanence that it seems not at all remarkable but quite natural for one of its postmasters to have been in office for fifty years. Hancock, named for Governor John Hancock, was first settled in 1764 but was not incorporated until after the Revolution. In 1800 the turnpike brought the outside world close to many hill towns and in Hancock an old brick tavern still recalls stage-coach days. This building, now owned by the local historical society and open to guests, contains some beautiful old china and furniture.

In Hancock there is a pretty little church similar to the one at Fitzwilliam. It has an oval window with crossed palms in

45. HANCOCK, NEW HAMPSHIRE. Now cows are "driven" to the common in a truck.

the pediment and a Paul Revere bell in the open belfry. The whole place—meetinghouse, tavern, white clapboarded houses, old stones in the graveyard—is so little changed from an earlier time that we felt no surprise at finding a cow there, though apparently cows are now "driven" to pasture differently. A cow in a truck would have surprised the founders of Hancock a good deal.

We like the bandstand on the Hancock common. Usually we think of these kiosks as having simply pushed their way out of the grass on some nineteenth-century night, but actually there was one on Boston Common before the Revolution. John Hancock gave the bandstand to Boston so the New Hampshire town that bears his name had good precedent for building one on its green.

Much loving care has been lavished on the painting of bandstands. Green and white may do for the rest of the village but the bandstand is likely to blossom in almost any color or combination of colors. Roof lines are varied too, sometimes suggesting the Taj Mahal, sometimes a Chinese Chippendale summerhouse. Now and then its roof makes a bandstand look like a small boy with a man's hat on, an endearing effect on the whole. Shingles crop out on bandstands, but not only on the roof. Often the jigsaw makes the whole building look as if it had been crocheted for a church fair.

We rather suspect that the architects of bandstands did not spend a great deal of time studying the designs of Sir Christopher Wren. Bandstands nevertheless pass on tradition, and were perhaps the forerunners of modern filling stations, as a glance at the corner one suggests.

The brassy sounds that once echoed from bandstands on summer evenings harmonized with their brightly painted roofs and frosted-wedding-cake fretwork. Somehow for a band concert a cornet always seems right. (We used to live near a man who practised his cornet solo every evening except Wednesdays and Saturdays, when he was playing in the band. We used to sit breathless at the concerts waiting for him to make again the same mistakes he had made on Monday, Tuesday, Thursday, and Sunday nights. He seldom disappointed us.)

Sousa's marches, all sounding much alike, were bandstand favorites. So was "The Last Rose of Summer." Since Indians had long ago disappeared from the green—except for an occasional visitor selling sweet-grass baskets—"Hiawatha" and "Tammany" could be thumped and brayed without making scalps tingle. Mosquitoes were the chief peril of the band concert. The lights attracted them. All the heroes of the village greens were not in the seventeenth century. Think of being a bald trombone player on a July evening in 1897!

Today band concerts are definitely not what they were. Selections from *Aida* replace "The Stars and Stripes Forever" and the whole place has been sprayed with D.D.T. There may not even be a roof over the band and we hear that this is considered an improvement because there is nothing to muffle the sound. Yet surely some sounds are better muffled. In any case, we often wish we could be again in a canoe on a lake—Norway Pond near the Hancock bandstand would do —in the year 1907 with strict instructions to start home when the band played "Good-Night, Ladies!"

Village greens like those at Hancock and Temple must look today very much as they have for half a century or more, but in busier places the old commons have often become little more than traffic circles. However, some of the larger towns have still kept their green spaces open. Newport's common is an elm-shaded stretch of green with a bandstand, fine early nineteenth-century houses, and a trim, well-kept brick hotel, all within a stone's throw of a crowded shopping center. Some miles further north, Lebanon has also succeeded in keeping its common as a peaceful place where people may stroll or rest from the heat of the day in the shade of great trees. The footpaths are now covered with asphalt, an unromantic material but probably an improvement since the original walks inclined to either mud or dust.

The first settlers of Lebanon came from Connecticut. Three soldiers who went from Connecticut to fight at Louisburg in

46. LEBANON, NEW HAMPSHIRE. A peaceful green remains in the midst of a busy town.

1758 came home through this part of New Hampshire and decided to return and settle. By that time, Indians were no longer the danger they had been earlier, so the settlement prospered from the start and progressed rapidly from log cabins to such beautiful houses as now face the common. The history of Lebanon has been peaceful.

There are many small industries in the town and one of the factories is on a corner of the common, but it has an air of Yankee tidiness about it that harmonizes with the white church, the brick library, and the old houses. The town was named for the earlier settlement in Connecticut from which most of the original settlers came. There the common was a mile long so a central green must have seemed a necessity for the new town. Now the new town is larger than the old one, which has not changed greatly since Rochambeau's troops drilled on that mile-long expanse in Revolutionary times.

Near the New Hampshire Lebanon and farther up the Connecticut River is New Hampshire's most beautiful green —College Green at Hanover, center of both town and college, for the green, though owned by the town is controlled by Dartmouth College. Hanover was only a struggling frontier settlement when the Reverend Eleazer Wheelock came there in 1770 to found his college "for the education & instruction of Youth of the Indian Tribes in this Land in reading, writing & all parts of learning which shall appear necessary and expedient for civilizing and christianizing Children of Pagans as well as in all liberal Arts and Sciences; and also of English youth and any others."

This last phrase was a fortunate one, for the "pagans" did not take readily to the arts and sciences. Perhaps their fathers felt as the Virginia Indians did when they were invited to send their sons to college. They replied that they appreciated the good will of the Virginians in making the suggestion but added:

We see that you mean to do us good and thank you heartily. But you who are wise, must know that different nations have different

ideas. . . . Several of our young men were brought up at Colleges in New England; they were instructed in all your sciences but when they came back to us, they were bad runners, ignorant of every means of living in the woods, unable to bear either cold or hunger, knew neither how to build a cabin, take a deer nor kill an enemy; spoke our language imperfectly; were therefore unfit for hunters, warriors, or councillors—they were therefore good for nothing.

We are however not the less obliged by your kind offer . . . and to show our grateful sense of it, if the gentlemen of Virginia will send us a dozen of their sons, we will take great care of their education, instruct them in all we know, and make men of them.

Dartmouth's student body soon became white and now the Indian tradition turns up chiefly in such places as the Harvard Stadium, often with a demonstration which shows that white men, in spite of defective education, can be good runners, endure cold, and embarrass the enemy considerably.

A schoolhouse was often one of the early buildings near a village green, but the first primitive ones disappeared long ago. The necessity for placing schools where children could reach them easily in all kinds of weather scattered little red schoolhouses at convenient cross roads rather than keeping them at the center of a town. Although free public schools played an important part in the history of New England towns, the schoolhouses themselves were not, like the meetinghouses, rebuilt over and over again in the same places.

It seems as if the school either left the green entirely or else became the real center of a town as at Hanover, Amherst, New Haven, or Andover, to mention but a few of the beautiful school and college greens of New England. When we visit Hanover and see the spacious green, elm-shaded in summer, white with blue shadows in winter, and enjoy the harmonious dignity of old and new buildings, we feel that the true solution of town planning has been found in this union of college and town. When we think of Amherst Common with the statue of Henry Ward Beecher presiding over it, or the setting of Bulfinch Hall at Andover, or "Paradise" on the campus of Smith College at Northampton, we wonder if all our New England commons might not still be beautiful if they could have been turned over to educational institutions. Too often the commons have been whittled down to meager triangles where grass fights a losing battle with plantains and ragweed, where the Honor Roll is already growing shabby and seems an indication that the town honors its soldiers only in an easy perfunctory way. Too often fine old houses are concealed beneath hideous, imitation brick siding or removed entirely to make way for structures of cement blocks. Too seldom are there groups like the Boston Common Society which recognize the value of our heritage and guard it for us and for generations to come.

One of the loveliest things about New Hampshire is the view of it from the Vermont side of the river, and one of the loveliest views is from Thetford Hill. Only a little way beyond the green a platform with benches has been built at the side of the road. We have never known whose hospitality it was that we accepted there but we are grateful for the times we ate our sandwiches in such a pleasant place and looked out across the river to the hills beyond, and we hereby state that no minute fragment of eggshell or scrap of paper was ever left behind us. The common at Thetford Hill is irregularly shaped and the whole place has a casual air as if the white houses, the church, and the elms had all come together by a happy accident.

The Old Congregational Church at the green there is one of the oldest in Vermont. It was built in 1787 and has been used for worship ever since. The town was in existence before that time and one of its men played an interesting part in the Revolution. On a cold night in the autumn of 1777, volun-

48. THETFORD HILL, VERMONT. Mountains rise behind one of the oldest commons in Vermont.

teers were called for at Ticonderoga to swim the two miles across Lake Champlain with dispatches. Ephraim Webster from Newbury and Richard Wallace from Thetford volunteered and accomplished their mission in spite of the bitterly cold water and the presence of the British fleet. The ships were so close that as they passed they could hear the watch on deck call out "All's well!"

For years after the Revolution there must have been many old soldiers in faded blue coats and cocked hats who sat in the sun on the village green and told stories to spellbound small boys. Perhaps Wallace was one of these. He never quite recovered from the effects of that cold night's work and we hope he often enjoyed the sunshine on warm May mornings or strolled up the hill to look down at Vermont and over at New Hampshire and feel that he had helped to win peace and prosperity for that fertile country where white villages flashed through the thin leaves.

There is still a schoolhouse near the green at Thetford Hill. By an unusual and sensible arrangement this old private school, Thetford Academy, also serves as the high school for the town; another instance of co-operation between school and community. In another part of Thetford is something we have never seen anywhere else—a green planted with pines instead of elms or maples. On the hot summer day when we stopped there the breeze through the pine branches sounded like the sea and the place stays green through the winter when other commons are bare. (This did not, however, shake our allegiance to elms!)

Newbury, where that other Revolutionary swimmer, Ephraim Webster, came from, is farther up the river than Thetford and stands closer to the water. It also has an old common, more formally designed than Thetford Hill's irregular green. On Newbury's long rectangle is a monument to Jacob Bayley, founder of the town and a sort of Ethan Allen from the eastern side of the Green Mountains. Once as Bayley was ploughing a field, he was in danger of being captured by the British. A friend sent him a message "The Philistines be upon thee, Samson!" and Bayley escaped across the river. Bayley once lived in part of what is now the Oxbow Antique Shop. The word oxbow refers not to an oxyoke but to the bends in the Connecticut River near Newbury where the stream loops in great wide shining curves through rich meadows.

Beyond the river and farther up in the hills is Chelsea, a town so fond of commons that it has two, running parallel to each other with the Orange County Court House at the head of one and the Congregational Church at the top of the other. These commons are set on sloping ground. It was more usual to select level land, probably with the drilling of troops in view, but Chelsea ignored any difficulties of the landscape. Maples make thick pools of shade on these commons and should be seen on what we always think of as "kingfisher days," the blue and gold days of late September when northern lights crackle across the night sky and the green grass of the common wears a silver veil of hoar frost in the morning. It is easy on such days to spot the kingfisher as he flies, gray-blue against leaves of flame and amber. Halcyon days the poets call them, naming them for the kingfisher, which is the Greek halcyon. We like the translation, for our kingfisher is a halcyon only in the sense that the white houses are Greek. Like our wooden Ionic columns and Doric pediments, he is Greek by adoption.

A summer evening is pleasant in Chelsea, too, especially if there are eight couples dancing a Plain Quadrille on the green, doing do-si-do and allemande left with rhythmical precision while their costumes defy every law of time and place. One man with a profile like George Washington's wears a Revolutionary costume—cocked hat, ruffled shirt, and knee breeches. Another is dignified in black broadcloth and stovepipe hat. Women's costumes vary from hoop skirts as wide as a door to velvet basques and wonderfully draped and padded bustles.

"They're wearing their ancestors' clothes," Ed Larkin, the best fiddler for miles around, explains between tunes. We notice that two of the dancers are decked out in feathers, buckskin, and wampum.

"Our ancestors were Indians," they assert solemnly.

Where, we wonder, were such relics preserved. Surely wigwams had no attics though in Vermont anything is possible! The grass on Vermont commons seems greener than grass anywhere else. Even in times of drought, dew falls heavily here on the cobwebs. On fine mornings, there are hundreds of them spread out like handkerchiefs on the green to dry. (Our grandson is the first child we ever saw who ate a lawnful of them.)

Most attractive among Vermont greens for beauty and historical significance is Bennington, the first town west of the Connecticut to receive a grant from Governor Benning Wentworth and named in his honor. New York claimed the part of Vermont west of the Green Mountains. New Hampshire claimed the eastern part. The federal government was willing to have the Hampshire Grants, as they were called, divided between the rival states. The British Government, even after the Revolution, had hopes of adding the territory to Canada. Vermont, however, succeeded in becoming first an independent republic and then in entering the federal union as the fourteenth state, bounded on the east by the Connecticut River and on the west by Lake Champlain.

Monument Avenue in Bennington recalls the days when Ethan Allen and his Green Mountain boys were fighting first against the "Yorkers" for the titles to the land they were clearing and then against the British for the independence of America. On this wide sloping green terrace the first settlers built their houses. Here, facing the green, where the first meetinghouse once stood, is the Old Burying Ground where lie both British and American soldiers killed in the Battle of Bennington. Beyond the graves rises the graceful steeple of the First Congregational Church, built by Lavius Fillmore, who was guided in the design by Asher Benjamin's book, *The Country Builder's Assistant*. Round-topped windows on the second story, Palladian windows above the door and in

49. BENNINGTON, VERMONT. One of the most beautiful of Vermont churches is near a Revolutionary battlefield.

the square part of the tower, oval windows in the octagonal lantern, add variety to the church and make it one of the most interesting in Vermont.

A bronze catamount on Monument Avenue marks the site of the Catamount Tavern where the Green Mountain Boys used to meet. It was formally designated the Green Mountain House, but its sign—a snarling catamount with open jaws—gave it its more familiar name. Before the Battle of Bennington, British officers sent a message to Stephen Fay, the landlord of the Catamount, ordering him to have dinner ready when they entered the town in triumph. As the British prisoners guarded by men in homespun limped down the road that hot August evening in their battle-stained scarlet, Fay welcomed them politely at his door and announced: "The dinner you ordered is ready, gentlemen."

The gray granite tower, which marks the site of the storehouse that Burgoyne lightheartedly ordered captured, dominates not only Monument Avenue but the whole countryside. It is the highest battle monument in the world, a shaft rising three hundred and six feet above the hill on which it stands. Four hundred and twelve steps take the visitor past thirty-four landings, on most of which he is glad to rest and look out over the green rolling country and the curves of the Walloomsac River to blue hills in the distance. The monument is exceptional not only for being the highest of all battle monuments but also—so far as we have heard—for being Vermont's only superlative.

Understatement is the Vermonter's natural idiom. His wife serves an angel cake so light and feathery it scarcely rests on the table, but she hands you a slice with a rueful face and remarks that "it didn't rise real well." Somehow, she says, she doesn't have good luck with this new flour. Her husband, when asked if he got as much maple syrup as he expected from his new sugar place answers, "No, not hardly," and after a pause for reflection adds mildly, "but I never thought I would." He says that his strawberries, each about the size of a small fillet mignon, sweet as honey and clover, and full of rich crimson juice are "pretty fair."

No Vermonter ever told us about the height of the Bennington Battle Monument. We learned about it from a foreigner from Massachusetts.

Oddly enough there is no statue of Ethan Allen among the monuments at Bennington. Allen's statue is in the portico of the State House above the Capitol Green at Montpelier. It is Seth Warner, the man who reinforced General Stark at Bennington, whose statue is at the head of Monument Avenue. Perhaps the choice reflects a natural Vermont liking for the quiet and reliable rather than the dashing and flamboyant.

Statues on New England commons are an unpredictable form of art. They range from the moving and spirited work of Augustus Saint-Gaudens in the Robert Gould Shaw Memorial on Boston Common to patented cast-iron figures of Civil War soldiers. The names of most of the sculptors are a well-kept secret but some at least were known in their day. Ethan Allen's statue at Montpelier was chiseled in marble by Larkin Goldsmith Mead, whose first piece of sculpture was presented to the public in a most dramatic fashion.. One bitterly cold New Year's morning, almost a century ago, the citizens of Brattleboro awoke to find on the small triangular plot in front of the schoolhouse an eight-foot winged figure made of snow and encased in shining ice. Mead with the help of two friends had worked all night, melting the dry snow to the right consistency, molding it according to his design, and glazing it with water. The water froze so rapidly and made such an effective coating that the figure stood there until the next thaw, which did not occur for some weeks. In the meantime Mead became famous. Several marble replicas of the Recording Angel, as he called it, were ordered. One of these is in All Souls' Church in Brattleboro, another in the cemetery at Westminster, Vermont.

Martin Milmore, a contemporary of Mead's had no such introductory advertising as the snow angel but in his short life he did a number of war memorials of which the Soldiers and Sailors Monument on Boston Common is the best known. The idea of this monument was so often imitated by anonymous stonecutters and metal founders that it became almost a stock design. The figure of Liberty, holding flag and shield, crowns the tall shaft of granite. At the corners are four realistic bronze sculptures—a soldier and a sailor and two seated female figures. There are also war memorials by Milmore at Keene, New Hampshire, and at Charlestown and Fitchburg, Massachusetts.

George Edwin Bissell, another nineteenth-century sculptor designed the Soldiers and Sailors Monument at Waterbury, Connecticut; the Standard Bearer at Winsted; and the figure, entitled Union, at Salisbury.

A young sculptor, Daniel Chester French, who began his work in a way almost as unconventional as Mead's received his first commission, a memorial to the heroes of the Revolution, when he was still inexperienced and could not afford to hire a model. Instead he used a plaster cast of the Apollo Belvedere, gave him long hair tied in a queue, a broad-brimmed hat with one side turned up, tight breeches, wrinkled boots, and rolled-up shirt sleeves. His left hand, held lower than that of the Apollo, is just leaving the handle of a plough, over which he has thrown his coat; his right holds his flint-lock. He looks fully competent to defend *The rude bridge that arched the flood* by which he stands—Concord's Minute-man.

A widely imitated monument, one characteristic of greens in hill villages, was John Quincy Adams Ward's figure of the Seventh Regiment Soldier in Central Park in New York. Ward prided himself on being a thoroughly American sculptor, on having learned his craft on this side of the Atlantic, and on using American models. At a time when the heroes of American history were often draped in Roman togas, he asserted, "I am not afraid of a frock coat and trousers." His realistic approach was a popular one and is reflected in many figures of private soldiers leaning on their muskets, figures which Ward never saw, much less designed. Sometimes sculptors tried to patent their statues, but as a rule it was the lesser men who sold statues as they might have soap. Men of the calibre of Ward submitted to having their ideas copied by the "gravestone men" and the makers of patented boiler-plate monuments.

Ward's best known Vermont work is on the State University's College Green at Burlington, a statue of Lafayette, showing him not as the young Revolutionary general but as an older man, possibly as he looked during his visit of 1825. At that time Lafayette laid the cornerstone of the Old Mill, the University's principal recitation hall. From the tower of this building there is a view across Lake Champlain to the Adirondacks on one side and across a wide sweep of country to the Green Mountains on the other—surely one of the finest distractions from study available to students on any college green. In Battery Park, Burlington has another green with a wonderful panorama of lake and mountain. Here men were trained and housed during the War of 1812 and here a battery of guns fought off three British ships of war. The cannon now in the park were used on the *Constellation* and on other United States ships in the Civil War.

There are many cannon and piles of cannon balls on the village greens as at Chester, New Hampshire. There are many granite shafts, too, and bronze tablets bearing the names of long dead soldiers, but some of the men who fought for the independence of America are buried in graves marked only by rough field stones without either name or date. We know a deserted village where, among roses and sheep laurel, the stones marking these almost forgotten graves can still be found. In two graves are soldiers of the Revolution who, we are told, were buried lying north and south instead of in the more usual east and west position. The story is that the men died of a swift and awful plague and the graves were placed in this way so that no one would ever dig there and set free the terrible infection. Even after all these years, we could still feel, under the hardhack and spirea that had grown above them, the sunken areas with head- and foot-stones pointing north.

In Vermont, graveyards are usually especially well cared for. Sometimes on an old farm the graveyard is the only garden, the only space carefully mown and shut away from cattle and hens. It may be surrounded by a high wall of neatly piled slate stones or by a hedge of clipped cedars.

"What is that white stone garden?" the three-year-old companion of one of our journeys asked us, pointing to a distant hillside where white stones, white fence, and white birches rippling in the sunshine marked all that remains of a settlement around an old common. Vermont commons often have a graveyard close at hand and the green and white pattern of the town is repeated in the marble tombstones, the white and green of syringa and bridal wreath, in plumes of white lilac, and in the greenish ivory of half-opened hydrangeas. Indeed in Bakersfield, Vermont, graveyard and green are actually one, the same maples shading them, the same white fence enclosing both.

We often find in New England graveyards what Mrs. Malaprop characterized as "a nice derangement of epitaphs." The remarks on these stones were sometimes ordered well ahead of time by those destined to lie beneath them. One of the most unusual of these monuments is behind a high cedar hedge at East Calais, Vermont. Few men have ever been so frank as Sidney Bennett was when he gave his order for his stone. Bennett was a peddler for many years, a fat man, almost stone-deaf and he used his deafness to advantage.

We heard of one visit he made to a farm kitchen where he threw himself into a chair and, in spite of being told that nothing was needed, tipped back comfortably and began to recite: "Now I have needles—needles as sharp as a lady's eyes, pins, tapes, some real pretty calicoes, just the thing for aprons when *he* comes around, combs . . ."

He tipped back further and further as he spoke. At "combs" his chair went over backwards with a crash, but he continued imperturbably from the floor: ". . . bodkins, buttons—mother of pearl, pants buttons, jet buttons to match your earrings—tape measures, sewing silk, red, blue, green, *and* pink . . ."

Of course, you had to buy from a man like that.

Bennett lived two miles from the village. The steep hill road from his house descends with hairpin turns into the valley, follows a twisting stream, and then curves around the edge of a precipice before climbing to another hillside. He directed that his coffin should be drawn to the graveyard by four black horses at a gallop—and so it was done.

On one side of his tombstone, a granite shaft, taller and more elaborate than the other stones around it, is cut the word Bennett; on the other, P. S. The Old Nuisance.

Everybody, he said, would know who *that* was.

When Vermonters drive through other states, they stop at graveyards near village greens and take notice of any stones that are sunken or tipping or have lichens growing on them. Then they think complacently of their own stones standing straight on neatly mown turf. Naturally they prefer to be buried in Vermont.

There was Albion Hull's grandmother, for instance. She was an exile, living across the Connecticut with her son-in-law and when she died, he had the bad judgment to have her buried in New Hampshire. Of course, her Vermont relatives could not stand that, so Albion went over, had the coffin disinterred and transported back across the river.

After it had been placed with due ceremony in the family lot in the graveyard across from the common, his wife asked, "Did you look at Grandma?"

"Yep."

"How did she look, Albion?"

Silence while Albion rallied his descriptive powers. His wife interrupted it by repeating, "Now, Albion, how *did* Grandma look?"

"Well," said Albion slowly and accurately, "I can't say as Grandma appeared real rugged."

50. WESTON, VERMONT. Old industries have been revived around this common.

CHAPTER *12*

Pattern Established

*I*n the old settlements like Billerica it might take two centuries for a village to emerge from the wilderness and
look as it does today. The green with its steepled meetinghouse appears so permanent, so unchanging that we assume
it is a stenciled pattern, easily repeated. Yet early records
of old towns indicate constant change. Sometimes a meetinghouse was enlarged, perhaps by cutting it down the center,
pulling the two halves apart, and building a new section in
between. The addition of a gallery or of a whole new front
may have been adequate for a time but sooner or later the
building was all pulled down and rebuilt, sometimes with the
old timbers, which were often used for more than one rebuilding. Eventually crude garrison houses, with overhanging second stories and floor boards ready to take up so women could
pour boiling water on Indians below, vanished and men began
thumbing over Asher Benjamin's *The Country Builder's Assistant* for doorway and chimney-piece designs. The tavern
was no longer a log hut with a floor of trodden earth but a
clean, well-furnished house, its parlor covered with scenic
paper showing the Monuments of Paris or the Bay of
Naples.

Towns passed ordinances forbidding "neat cattle, horses
and horse kind to run at large without a keeper" and finally

banished them from the common. Then, after a while the blacksmith shop disappeared—sometimes becoming a shoppe and serving vegetable plates—and at last even the stone drinking trough is gone.

"Turn right at the green where the drinking trough used to be," were the directions we received for reaching a certain house. We followed them conscientiously, turning where we would have stopped to let our horse drink in the shade of a big elm—if we had had a horse—and found the place we sought.

Elms have been growing taller and throwing deeper shadows while buildings have been appearing and reappearing. Eighteenth-century prints usually show old commons looking barer than they do now. At first, trees were the settlers' natural enemies. Farms were granted on condition that a certain number of acres be cleared of trees before a certain date. Later, trees were planted on the greens and now they are earnestly cherished and advised to see their tree surgeon twice a year.

The roads leading to the common have changed sometimes even more than the village itself, especially in wintertime, now that sleigh bells are silent. The snow used to be packed down hard for sleighs with wooden rollers. Now it is ploughed away. At Bennington, during the Revolution, the Overseer of the Tories was ordered to send out ten of his charges to tread the snow down on the road to Wilmington. Three days provisions were issued to them and they were to be marched back again "at all convenient speed."

We can remember riding in a sleigh to which the horse was harnessed at one side so that he broke the trail for one of the runners. We remember, too, the sleigh tipping over when the other runner met an unexpected obstacle and the resulting discussion as to whether it was better to fall on someone or be fallen upon. We were underneath and our companion pointed out that we had the nice soft snow to fall on whereas she was jolted by landing on us. In any event our ribs mended nicely in about a fortnight.

When the snow melted, paths around the common were quagmires. At last, asphalt was put down. While fresh, it was deliciously soft and held marks where children spun around it on their heels—sometimes forever. When the asphalt hardened, it provided an excellent surface for roller skating, hopscotch, and for writing, usually untruthfully, that Billy loves Polly. Lawn mowers became popular, especially with the wives of the men who pushed them. The men were often of the opinion that cows and sheep did a good enough job of cropping the greens and should be brought back.

As the nineteenth century progressed, houses changed inside, even if to the passer-by they looked much as they always had. As the owners, being New Englanders never threw anything away, the rooms naturally became very crowded. Probably no rooms ever had quite the bleak, polished elegance of the eighteenth-century rooms that are now museums—rooms preserved in aspic, they always seem to us. After all, human beings once occupied them and presumably littered them with riding crops, gloves, snuff boxes, pipes, teething rings, old letters, hobby horses, scent bottles, dolls, unpaid bills, toddy glasses, samples of chintz, and packs of cards. Doubtless boys were rebuked for whittling and bringing in birds' nests and for emptying pockets of their interesting burden of portable property on the Turkey carpet. Possibly their fathers cleaned guns and left the rags around on mahogany card tables. Certainly their sisters embroidered those sad pictures in which willows and anemic ladies wept eternally over tombstones so there must have been stray threads of silk caught on the chair cushions. Lacquering trays and boxes was another elegant accomplishment and one capable of cluttering up considerable space as any of our relatives who has seen us at work can testify.

Perhaps all these activities did not produce rooms so untidy as those of various eighteenth-century engravings, where spinning wheels jostle pewter teapots, torn shirts hang on bedposts, and little dogs steal mutton bones conveniently left on chairs. Yet certainly the early New England rooms did not have the museum look of having been painfully made neat for company that never came.

Probably the rooms in the old houses around the greens were never so crowded as they were in the last half of the nineteenth century. Women at that time seemed to take pride in making houskeeping as difficult as possible. They starched everything—shirts, lace curtains, pillow shams, petticoats, until they seemed to have an independent existence and took up all the space they could. Whalebone lurked nearly everywhere, bolstering up weak-minded fabrics. The best thing you could say about a dress was that it "stood alone." Yet softness was popular too, especially in something normally hard, such as a table. Much loving care was expended in padding tables and sewing ball fringe around the edge of the coverings. Any woman who could get hold of a piece of chenille was happy.

Nineteenth-century housewives loved to put things on top of other things—antimacassars on chairs, shawls on pianos, scarfs over screens, doilies on whatnots. They loved feathers, in beds, on bonnets, in dusters, and in Japanese jars on the mantelpiece. It was a stuffy period, but it was a comfortable one. And for the first time in history, the houses on the commons were warm in winter!

Of course, kitchens always had a certain amount of warmth, although most of the heat from the four-foot logs burning in the great fireplaces went up the huge chimneys. We know an old Vermont house where there is still a semicircular mark on the floor around the fireplace. An old man who spent his boyhood there explained that the color of the floor was different because the frost used to lie on the floor outside the range of the heat.

"We'd hang sides of beef on the wall over there!" he explained. "They'd keep froze good and hard all winter. Handier than them freezer lockers, I snum."

Kitchens in houses that are now museums have most nearly the old look. It is possible to imagine, in such places as the Farrar-Mansur House at Weston, Vermont that the mistress of the tavern has just left her kitchen with its many utensils washed and put away for the afternoon and that she will return and use her brass and pottery, iron and pewter when she cooks supper.

Weston is a town which demonstrates that the old pattern can still produce a satisfying community life. Vrest Orton and other Weston citizens have proved that if in rebuilding, men use the pioneer spirit their ancestors used in building, they can today achieve some of the same results. Old industries have been revived and new ones started around the circular, maple-shaded green. There is the Ortons' country store, a friendly meeting place and a flourishing enterprise, a mill where whole grains are ground slowly in the old-fashioned way, looms for hand-woven tweeds, a woodworking shop where great chunks of native hardwoods are turned into bowls, and an abandoned church, which has been converted into an attractive small theater.

The first town meeting in Weston was held in the Farrar-Mansur House in 1800. Although it is a museum now, it is still a community house, too, and has an air of vitality often lacking in old houses open to the public. Country dancing still goes on in the upstairs ballroom where the walls have been newly decorated in old patterns. One mural shows a dance in which the faces, figures, and costumes of the dancers have been taken from the portraits and daguerreotypes of Weston people.

Towns like Weston, which were settled at the end of the eighteenth century, did not begin as clusters of log huts inside a stockade and develop slowly into settlements of dignified houses of white clapboard and red brick. If log houses were built at all, they were used merely as temporary shelters. The pattern of green, meetinghouse, square white dwellings was clear in the minds of the settlers as they plodded along beside their oxen with brass kettles, spinning wheels, foot stoves, four-posters, and highboys piled up on sledges. The highboy in our own bedroom was brought to Vermont on an ox sledge over a blazed trail. It was called the Lightening Ridge Road because just where we shift into low gear now, the load was lightened and the oxen made a second trip with what had been removed.

At the end of the eighteenth century men knew how a town should look: the one they left behind had been pulled down and rebuilt until it satisfied some inner sense of beauty combined with practicality. The new settlement must be like the old one only placed in a country where the soil was rich, where streams ran swiftly to turn millstones and drive saws, where there was plenty of land for men who had the strength to clear it, and women who had the courage to follow them.

The link between the old town and the new one was often expressed in the name of the new settlement. The mother and daughter relationship is clear in Haverhill, New Hampshire, Rutland and Barre, Vermont, all of which are named for Massachusetts towns. This duplication of names is often confusing and we sometimes think of it as a lack of originality in the settlers, a sign of a perfunctory attitude in choosing the name as if they had been too lazy to think of another. Nothing could be further from the truth as the naming of Barre, Vermont, shows.

Barre was originally called Wildersburgh but the inhabitants decided that this name was "uncouth" and determined to change it to something more musical. At the town meeting where the question was decided, two men from Massachusetts, Thompson from Holden and Sherman from Barre, each proposed the name of his native town with such enthusiasm that words led to blows, one of them so effective that Sherman was knocked flat, and for a moment it seemed as if the town would be named Holden. However, Sherman succeeded in pulling Thompson down to the floor with him and as they rolled around slugging, kicking, and tussling, Sherman got in a lucky punch and Thompson subsided into a long, limp silence.

Sherman struggled to his feet. "There, b'God, the name's Barre!" he gasped.

He was right.

Often the connection with an earlier settlement is not so

51. STURBRIDGE, MASSACHUSETTS. From this settlement men left to establish new communities in Vermont.

obvious because the new town is given the name of its leading citizen. Nevertheless, the pattern of the older town can be traced in the new one. An example of one of these hidden mother and daughter relationships is in the tie between Sturbridge, Massachusetts, and Craftsbury Common, Vermont.

The country around Sturbridge was explored as early as 1633 by two men from Plymouth. They were led to the discovery of a graphite mine by meeting the Indians of the region and becoming curious about the source of the black substance with which the Indians disfigured their faces. The vein of graphite was found at a place appropriately called Black Hill and attempts at mining it were made but were not successful, so Sturbridge developed like other towns in the region into an agricultural community around a wide common. Like other towns, it used water power to grind grain and saw wood and later had several manufacturing enterprises—a cotton mill, a shoe factory, and what is still a prosperous auger and bit factory.

The first permanent settlement of the town was in 1729. Sturbridge played its part in the Revolution. Sturbridge people still look across the spacious shady common and see the walls of the cemetery which were built by four companies of Revolutionary soldiers, each company building a side. The leading citizen of the town, Colonel Ebenezer Crafts, equipped and drilled his own cavalry regiment in the early part of the war and later served under Washington. Like many other Revolutionary officers, Colonel Crafts had been an inn keeper. In 1771 he had built the Public House, the rambling, roomy old tavern which still faces Sturbridge Common and still welcomes visitors in motor cars as it once did those in stagecoaches.

Inflation and depression followed the Revolution, as they have other wars, and times were hard in Sturbridge. One evening in 1780, Colonel Crafts called his neighbors together. He had decided, he said, to sell his inn and try his fortunes in a new country. Of the sixty men who crossed the common to the Public House that night, many agreed to follow him to found a new settlement in Vermont.

In November of that year, Governor Chittenden granted land in what is now Craftsbury to the colonel and his followers. The charter divided the proposed township into one hundred and forty-four lots, each half a mile square. Two lots were to be held by each of sixty-five proprietors on condition that five acres of land must be cleared and a house built within three years. The remaining lots were to be the property of the town. One of these lots, the proprietors agreed with the pattern of Sturbridge in mind, would be for a meetinghouse and a common, which was to be as near the center of the town as possible.

The men who left Sturbridge for Craftsbury had to get through some two hundred and fifty miles into what was almost a wilderness. There had been a military road built in that part of Vermont during the Revolution. The pioneers followed this road, clearing away branches and bushes with their axes where the path was choked. They reached the end of their journey in 1788 while Vermont was still an independent republic. The motto was:

> *We owe no allegiance,*
> *We bow to no throne,*
> *Our rule it is law,*
> *And the law is our own.*

As they chopped their way towards their new town in the hills, Colonel Crafts and his party doubtless carried with them a picture of an open green common with white houses and a meetinghouse, of a comfortable inn, of elm shadows, perhaps even of a neat white fence.

It was the custom in the settlement of these towns in the Vermont wilderness to make the journey in late winter or early spring while there was still snow on the ground. Ox-drawn sledges were easier to manage on snow than wheeled vehicles over rocks and through mud. The settlers would work all summer clearing land and building shelters and then re-

52. CRAFTSBURY COMMON, VERMONT. On a high plateau in the Green
Mountains, this old common is today the scene of ball games,
band concerts, and sugaring-off parties.

turn to their homes in the south—Massachusetts is a place of tropical languor to a Vermonter—for the winter. In 1791 several Sturbridge families made the trip to Vermont. Some of the men travelled on snowshoes and dragged their families on hand sleds. Colonel Crafts cut a branch of a Balm of Gilead tree in Claremont, New Hampshire, to use on his oxen. He planted the whip in his garden at Craftsbury and it grew into a tree which was a landmark for many years.

The town was formally organized in 1792 and soon afterwards the common lot was surveyed and laid out. Like the old green at Sturbridge, it was used for training soldiers. The militia of the whole county used to drill there on a piece of ground forty rods square but later reduced by the sale of building lots. In 1807 the common was leased for pasturage in return for being cleared of tree stumps, graded, and seeded.

The meetinghouse was built in 1802. Even at that late date the church expected to control the worldly behavior of its members. Though Colonel Crafts was a leader in the church as well as in the town, he was not exempt from moral censure. A church record of 1800 reads: "Col. Ebenezer Crafts was, sometime in the month of June last, guilty of the scandalous sin of using profane language and also of saying to Mr. Daniel Kelsey, 'Go with me' with such threatening words as gave evidence to fight the said Kelsey."

From the evidence, Colonel Crafts would have made a formidable opponent. He is said to have been so strong that he could lift a barrel of cider and drink from the bunghole. The record describes no actual conflict and we cannot help suspecting Mr. Kelsey of telling tales to the deacons instead of accepting the Colonel's invitation to "go with" him. At another time Colonel Crafts was summoned before the church but failed to appear, even after repeated commands, and was excommunicated. Evidently the church needed him more than he needed its discipline, for he was reinstated and became clerk and moderator.

The common at Craftsbury has always been the center of the town's life. Elms planted there in 1799 as a tribute to

George Washington still stand, but it is more than a place of memories, or like some commons, simply a piece of well-mown grass, convenient for an honor roll. Like the old common at Sturbridge, where marks of baseball show on the grass, Craftsbury Common is still used and enjoyed by the people of the town. It, too, has worn spots made by Sunday ball games and the band still gives concerts in the bandstand. There is an annual sugaring-off party when Craftsbury children and grownups too, have all the crisp, lacy sugar-on-snow they can eat and then devour pickles, so they can eat more sugar.

No Vermont common seems to us so beautiful as this one. It is encircled first by a neat white fence, within which are shining houses and brilliant flower gardens and the smoothest of green lawns. Beyond, the country rolls away in wide fields and wooded hills with small white farm houses and big red barns on the slopes. The hills become mountains and melt from dark green to purple to pale blue and at last fade into the sky. Many greens have the charm of compactness, of being safely shut away from the world outside. Craftsbury is different. It has an atmosphere of freedom, of space, of wind blowing off mountain tops.

We feel that, like the old independent republic, it can still state:

> *Our rule it is law*
> *And the law is our own.*

Like most village commons, it commemorates war in times of peace. A granite block is a memorial to the men of three wars. We like to think of Craftsbury, too, as a monument to that robust, pugnacious, sometime profane, and "scandalous" sinner, Colonel Ebenezer Crafts.

Often it seems as if the pattern of the village green, worked out with so much hardship in places like Billerica, carried with so much courage to settlements like Craftsbury, was completed only to be tossed aside. Prosperity often whittles down a New England common to just the place where you take the bus. Yet prosperity does not always win. Only a short time ago, in Leominster, Massachusetts, a bus company had actually started work on the foundations of a waiting room placed on the green in the center of the city when some one brought out the old deed by which the First Congregational Society granted the common to the town. In the deed was this proviso: "That said land is not to be used for any other purpose than that of a common, not to be applied to purposes of tillage or have buildings placed on it, but the Town may enclose it with a light fence to protect ornamental herbage or trees."

So Leominster Common remains what it was intended to be—a place where people can rest in the sunshine or walk in the shade.

The neatest and most picturesque commons do not always give the most pleasure. Sometimes they seem a little like those handsomely upholstered chairs with ropes across them in museums. Chippendale was a great cabinet maker and so was Sheraton, but no chair with a rope across it ever took the weight off weary feet. Velvety grass is an attractive feature of a common and so are white houses and arching elms but unless the place is used, it may become as prettily unreal as the backdrop of a village scene in a nineteenth-century play.

We like to see a green like the one at Bath, Maine, where the grass is not too precious to be walked on and no one would mind if you skipped stones in the pond, where the trees are like fountains and the fountain is like a tree, where it is all right to lie on the ground or to sit primly on a bench or even to go fishing.

A town that still uses its common in an interesting way is Whitingham, Vermont. Originally the village was built around a common at the top of a two thousand foot hill with a view across Sadawga Lake to the Green Mountains. Because the water supply was inadequate, the town was moved down the hill and the old village was deserted. Instead of letting the common grow up into woods again, the town has kept it for a picnic and recreation ground. There are swings and rings, fireplaces—and the wood for them—benches and tables, and a baseball field.

The common is busiest in Old Home Week when there is a baseball game and a supper with every kind of pie known to woman. Women are restless about pies but men are conservative. Once a Vermont cook was asked what kind of pie she had made for dinner.

She replied, "Deep-dish, open-face, crossbar and kiver-top—and all APPLE."

The relief on the faces of the men at this announcement was a pretty sight. We heard a Vermonter say thoughtfully and pityingly as he looked down on the city of Boston from the Custom House tower: "I don't expect there's a dozen women in the place that serve apple pie twice a day."

We did not dare to contradict him. Indeed we feared he was right. However, though Bostonians may have forsaken this tradition, in some ways they have kept others. As we cross the Common on Christmas Eve, for instance, and see the lights come out on the great Christmas tree, we are enjoying something our Puritan ancestors would never have allowed. We do not follow their prejudice in this matter nor do we any longer regard the Common as a suitable place for public whippings or hangings. Yet we do respect the old principle, brought here from England by those first Americans, of the common ownership of land for the benefit of all the people of a community. Boston Common demonstrated so clearly the value of the pattern that it was carried through New England and appears, though with many variations of surrounding buildings and natural settings, over and over again in all the states. The commons were not acquired without difficulty and it has often been a struggle to keep them, simply in the sense of keeping them from being built on, from being reduced by encroaching traffic. It has required civic effort to keep the grass green and smoothly mown and trees pruned. In the larger sense too, as symbolized by the monuments of many wars, the commons have not without

53. BATH, MAINE. The green is spacious and the grass not too precious
to be walked on.

difficulty been kept as places for free men to walk. Because it is easy to pass by the commons without realizing the sacrifices for which they stand, we record here a few names from the hundreds on the Honor Roll that stands on Boston Common. These men, like thousands of others whose names may be read on New England village greens, died, in some measure at least, so that these peaceful elm-shaded spaces might remain as they had always known them.

Altieri, Borowski, Lung Sung Chin, Dempsey, Edstrom, Ferrara, Gallagher, Hesselbarth, Isburg, Janakas, Kelly, Leblanc, McEachern, Napoli, O'Toole, Piazza, Quinn, Retzsch, Smith, Troxil, Urquhart, Versiackas, Washington, Youdowitz, Zalewski—all Americans.

CHAPTER *13*

Who Lived on Village Greens?

W hat kind of people lived around New England village greens? It is easy to say all kinds, and let it go
at that. Of course, there have been misers and spendthrifts,
wise men and fools, gentlewomen and shrews, honest men and
rogues. It is impossible to point to any one man and say:
"There goes a typical New Englander—there is no other
kind."

Still there are a few fairly definite New England characteristics. John Dunton, a young Englishman, who travelled
here in the eighteenth century observed them when he was
writing about the landlord of the inn at Ipswich, Massachusetts:

As to his stature 'tis inclining to tall: and as to his aspect, if all the
lineaments of a sincere and honest-hearted man were lost out of this
world, they might be retrieved by looking in his face. He's one of
those whose bounty is limited by reason, not by ostentation: and to
make it last he deals discreetly; as we sowe our land not by the
sack but by the handful. He is so sincere and upright that his words
and his meaning never shake hands and part but always go together.
His mind is always so serene that that thunder but rocks him to sleep
which breaks other men's slumbers. . . . He is not much given to talk
though he knows how to do it as well as any man. He loves his friend
and will do anything for him except it be to wink at his faults of

which he is always a severe reprover. He is so good a husband that he is worthy of the wife he enjoys. and would even make a bad wife good by his example.

This innkeeper did not have to set a good example to a bad wife. Dunton writes further:

Her stature is of middle size fit for a woman. . . . When she was about 18—perhaps there was never a face more sweet and charming— nor could it well be otherwise for now at 33 all you could call sweet and ravishing is in her Face; which it is as great a pleasure to behold as a perpetual sunshine with no clouds at all; and yet all this sweet- ness is joined with such attractive vertue as draws all to a certain dis- tance and there detains them with reverence and admiration, none ever daring to approach her nigher or having power to go further off. She's so obliging courteous and civil as if those qualities were only born in her. . . . So good a wife is she that she frames her nature to her hus- band's. . . . Her household is her charge. . . . Her pride is to be neat and cleanly and her thirst not to be Prodigal.

We are afraid she is less typical than her husband. Still there are traits we recognize—the neatness, for one.

We remember a Vermont couple whose pride was also to be neat. One afternoon Abel went up to the shed chamber to get something Susan wanted. When he came down he said, "Susan, while I was up there, I saw a fly."

"All right, Abel," said Susan. "I'll be right up."

Stinginess to phrase it indelicately—Mr. Dunton skirts this subject politely—often goes along with neatness. Like jealousy, which is said always to be born of love but not to die with it, the thirst not to be prodigal often seems to arise with neatness. Yet it can also exist for its own sake. Our grandmother knew two rich old bachelors. Each had a hobby. One collected string, boxes of it; the other collected old boots, sometimes odd ones, by the barrel. Each had a bureau of a peculiar type: the top drawer was deeper than the others and the front let down to form a desk. The neigh- bors claimed that the brothers ate their meals at these bureau-desks so they could shut the drawers in case a friend

54. CHESTER, NEW HAMPSHIRE. What kind of people lived around these quiet greens?

dropped in unexpectedly. The familiar expression, "Take a lot, take two," was attributed to one of them in a spasm of generosity while passing a bowl of popcorn.

Of another New England family we have heard it said that "the Allisons always eat rotten apples." It seems that Grandma Allison went over the apples as soon as they were brought in and served at once any that had bad spots. By the time these were gone, a few more had softened up, so the family ate those and, proceeding in this way, managed to have a supply of the same kind all winter.

Some of this carefulness goes back, no doubt, to early days of privation, the Plymouth days of the five grains of parched corn; to the fact that New England was never a rich part of the country. Much of the land was unfit for cultivation. The fields were full of rocks, the climate full of temperament. There were no rich mineral deposits, no oil, no wide plains that could be ornamented with amber grain. New Englanders had to conquer the world they found by their own skill of hand and brain.

It is often said that four maxims have made New England great:

> Eat it up.
> Wear it out.
> Make it do.
> Go without.

In obedience to these counsels New Englanders eat the last fish ball, whether they want it or not, "to save it." Maple highboys, the plates from Audubon's *Birds of America,* fiddle-back chairs, copper luster pitchers, glass paper weights, blue and white coverlets—these still exist there because some one cared for them and saved them.

Of course, things of less obvious value were saved, too, but sometimes they also proved useful. We know a woman whose son went into the army and who, when he had been promoted to take charge of the maps for his company, wrote home that at night in the field he needed some way of working on them without showing a light. At the time he was working kneeling down with a raincoat over his head. What he needed, he said, was a small portable dark room. It had to hold a map board of certain dimensions, let no light through, be waterproof, and lightweight, have some means of illumination, be rigid in use but readily collapsible. From these specifications his mother proceeded to construct a map illuminator, sometimes known as Hugh's Secret Weapon. As she is a New Englander, she found the materials, which included an umbrella, in attics—her own attic and her neighbors' attics, for neighborliness is still practiced around village greens. In fact, one of the things that New Englanders keep the longest is old friends.

The wear-it-out maxim is always in operation in New England. "I simply wait seven years and I am in style again," we heard someone state serenely the other day. "They say skirts will be longer." But fashion still had a few years to go before catching up with her present costume, we observed.

The make-it-do formula is at the bottom of a great deal of Yankee ingenuity. The advice to "go without" is still followed, but in a way not always recognized. New Englanders do go without a great many things, but often for the sake of some larger generosity. They drive in twenty-five-year-old Pierce Arrow cars but endow hospitals; wear shawl-collared dinner jackets but buy old masters for their city's museum; cherish ancient Inverness capes and eat baked beans for supper Saturday nights so as to help some boy through college.

Industriousness is a general New England trait. Women feel embarrassed if they are found reading a book in the daytime, unless it is a book heavy enough to be laid on a table, in which case they are doing research and all is well. If they are knitting something, no matter how abrasive, it is virtuous. Writing is considered rather an idle habit because it is generally done sitting down and there is little to show as a result but inky fingers. Composing music is also a matter for apology, but playing a musical instrument, preferably a large one, is commendable because of the obvious physical activity.

A housewife who is making a good chicken pie feels superior to all artists, and perhaps rightly so. Good cooks are rare, though less so around village greens than the casual traveller might think, for good cooking is found in homes, not at hot dog stands.

New Englanders take a mournful pride in how terrible the weather is—how cold the winters, how hot the summers, how big the hail stones, how deep the flood, how fierce the wind. They love calamity. Those who didn't went away long ago.

Yet the exiles come back, or their children or grandchildren do.

A New England friend of ours once realized her ambition and got to California. She loved everything, the sunshine, the Pacific, the pepper trees and palms, even the sidewalk orators in Los Angles. One day she was listening to an exceptionally eloquent one when she noticed that his audience was deserting him and moving across the street, so she went too. There in a shopwindow was a large poster showing Park Street in Boston, the familiar steeple, a piece of the Common, the dome of the State House, and incidentally her own office window.

Above it a sign read: "Fulfill the Dream of a Lifetime: Visit New England."

At first it seemed funny. Here she had saved for years to get to California and was immediately implored to start saving again and go back to Boston. Then she began to hear the comments around her: "My mother came from there. My grandfather used to have a farm in Concord. I have a cousin . . ." Genealogies were exchanged and at last a man who had been gazing silently at the poster scene said: "I used to work for a publisher on that street. That's their office right there," and he pointed to a doorway. "I drew pictures for them," he said, and then added wistfully, "I was there just once."

Our friend could bear it no longer.

"I work for them too," she said, "that's *my* office window."

If she had revealed that she was Priscilla Alden herself, the sensation could not have been greater, she says, and somehow she saw Boston Common as she had never seen it before, partly perhaps because she and the illustrator and the man whose grandfather farmed at Concord were all on the edge of tears.

Perhaps when we list the essential elements of the village green—the white meetinghouse, the old houses, shadows on smooth turf, the tracery of elm branches against the sky, we may feel, as Henry James did, that the total impression of the green is deeper than these items, taken separately, seem to warrant. Perhaps if our sum does not come out right, it is because we overlook the many people whose roots are there. We must take into account, too, that in many places outside New England where people walk or rest, however briefly, in the shade of an open space common to all citizens, they share the New England heritage, for the concept of the village green did not stay in New England but travelled across the country along with New Englanders.

It may be only a green triangle left by branching roadways; it may be a smooth-shaven oblong barely large enough to hold monuments to dead soldiers; it may be a common roughly mown with the scythe in some sleepy hill town where boys play ball after supper; or it may be some great city park, complete with golf links and tennis courts, rare trees, gardens, and lakes, where thousands of people go for recreation.

Emerson said: "The creation of a thousand forests is in one acorn." He might have added that the grass on all village greens came from the same seed. Wherever we find green space and trees, the common property of a town or city, we find a monument to the self-sacrifice and vision of those Americans who, in hewing the first towns out of the wilderness, always devoted some part of their strength to the common welfare of all the people.

55. BREWSTER, MASSACHUSETTS. In winter and summer, elm branches trace beautiful patterns against the sky.

CHAPTER *14*

Greens to Enjoy

*W*e should like to discuss many more New England greens and commons than this book would hold, and show their pictures as well. But all we can do is to include enough of them to indicate the way they have developed—sometimes as a breathing space in a busy city, sometimes keeping the compact sheltered air of an eighteenth-century village.

Almost everyone will be disappointed that some favorite green is not shown. We are, too, so in addition to the greens discussed, we are listing here many more. In all we have considered in this book over one hundred and fifty greens and commons. We have selected them either because they are of attractive appearance, have beautiful meetinghouses or other handsome old buildings near by, or because interesting historical events are connected with them.

It is worth while turning aside from main roads to visit these quiet greens, and to do so at leisure. No one who is in a hurry will get the feeling of the old towns clustered around them. It is better to see two or three greens—to read the inscriptions on the bronze plates on the boulders or on the granite monuments, to visit the local historical societies, to look up at the belfries of churches, perhaps to hear the notes of a bell cast by Paul Revere, to walk in the shade of the elms, to imagine the stagecoach rolling up to the tavern—than to dash from one to another, trying to see them all. There are hundreds of green oases in New England, each with a long tradition. To know even one well is to enrich our sense of the past.

CONNECTICUT

A book might be written on Connecticut greens alone. This list is merely an introduction to the subject.

Bolton Center

Eighteenth- and early nineteenth-century houses cluster around a green where, in the Revolution, Rochambeau's army camped on the march from Newport to the Hudson.

Branford (Illustrated)

A triangular green of generous size is enjoyed by the townspeople. Trinity Episcopal Church, Town Hall, and Court House face on the pleasant expanse.

Brooklyn

General Israel Putnam once kept a tavern here and left his plough standing in the field when he went to join the Continental Army.

Cheshire

Near the green is the Congregational Church, one of the many beautiful Connecticut churches which follow the design of David Hoadley's church at Milford.

Colchester

Another place where Rochambeau's army camped is not far from the green at Colchester. An old stage-coach tavern, gravestones with interesting inscriptions, and fine gambrel-roofed houses are all worth stopping to see.

Coventry

In the minister's house near the green, Nathan Hale prepared for college.

Durham

The green here is among wooded hills where two rival churches competed in building the higher steeple. The spire that won the contest was blown over and landed, point down, on the church roof.

East Haddam (Illustrated)

A bell cast in 815 A.D. hangs in the old church tower in this village where Nathan Hale once taught in a little red schoolhouse.

Fairfield

A busy town which nevertheless has preserved its old meetinghouse and village green. The Post Road (U.S. 1) by-passes both.

Glastonbury

A prosperous suburb of Hartford preserves a variety of old houses, one possibly of seventeenth-century origin.

Greenfield Hill

This part of the town of Fairfield has a green which was once a training ground for Revolutionary soldiers—ninety-eight are buried in the graveyard—a building where a store was kept for two centuries, and some handsome old houses.

Guilford
>One of the most beautiful of New England towns has a wide green, tall elms, a church in the Greek Revival style, and more than a hundred old houses along its streets.

Huntington Green
>The site of the early settlement of the town of Shelton has an old church and early houses, some of them of the salt-box type.

Litchfield (Illustrated)
>Here is a pattern for the typical New England village green and the scene of a famous stove feud.

Manchester
>The old idea of the central green for the civic center has been used here in the present century.

Manchester Green
>One of the many old taverns where Washington was entertained is near this green.

Meriden
>The long oblong green, once a training ground for Revolutionary soldiers, has a memorial to them.

Middlebury (Illustrated)
>Nowhere is there a greater feeling of serenity than on this smooth lawn under the elms.

Milford
>Palisades once enclosed a plot of land a mile square, protecting the town from Indian raids. The green is still almost half a mile long and is said to have been cut to the size and shape of the hull of the *Great Eastern,* the ship used in laying the Atlantic Cable.

The Congregational Church, designed by David
Hoadley, has been a model for many Connecticut
churches of the early nineteenth century. Features of
the design, often copied, are the portico with Ionic
pillars and the graceful spire with open belfry.

New Haven (Illustrated)

The green has been the civic and religious center of
the town since 1638.

Old Lyme

The delicate spire of the Congregational Church
rises above a green triangle where patriotic citizens
burned tea at the time of the Revolution.

Sharon

The long mall is bordered by well-preserved old
houses, some of them of eighteenth-century brick-
work. In the nineteenth century a Civil War monument and a clock tower of gray granite were built.

South Woodstock (Illustrated)

Elms were planted here to celebrate the Battle of
Lexington. They still shade the green.

Southington

The Congregational Church here is another of those
patterned after David Hoadley's church in Milford.

Vernon Center Green

The church here departs from the Hoadley pattern.
It has a square tower with bull's-eye windows and a
sharp tapering spire.

Waterbury

Hundreds of people enjoy this old green every day
as they wait for the bus.

Wethersfield

This early settlement, now a suburb of Hartford, has a common at one end of the town and a green at the other, shaded by immense elms and maples, which flourish on soil that once formed the bed of the Connecticut River. There are fine examples of seventeenth- and eighteenth-century architecture here.

Windham (Illustrated)

Few greens seem so untouched by today's hustle and bustle as Windham's with its well-preserved old buildings and fine trees.

Windsor

Here is another Connecticut settlement, which retains its old pattern of a central green in spite of the encroachments of modern living. Broad Street Green is in the business area and across the Farmington River is Palisado Green. The buildings near these greens range from the seventeenth to the twentieth centuries.

Wolcott

This is a quiet village where the green is at the top of a hill. Bronson Alcott, better known for his life in transcendentalist Concord, was born near by.

Woodbury

The Masonic Hall, known as King Solomon's Temple, dominates Woodbury's green from a high ledge at the south end. There are also interesting old churches and a soldier's monument.

Woodstock Hill

A beautifully proportioned Congregational Church, an old academy, and a tavern where stagecoaches used to stop are near this peaceful green.

In Rhode Island, the pattern of the village green is not nearly so much a matter of course as in Connecticut and Massachusetts. The reasons for this difference between Rhode Island and her neighbors to the south and north lie partly, as we noted earlier, in the religious attitudes of the settlers of the various colonies. The region where William Blaxton found relief from the society of the Lord Brethren (whom he found no more congenial than the Lord Bishops in England), the place where Roger Williams escaped the oppression of the Puritans, and where Quakers were tolerated was not likely to produce a tightly knit community grouped around a meeting house and governed by it in every detail of conduct.

Rhode Island's sandy lowlands close to the sea are more hospitable to clambakes than to tree-shaded lawns and, as in other places, the sea tended to draw men's interests away from compact living and out to the world beyond. Even inland, the country did not seem to lend itself readily to the village-green type of town planning. Rhode Island early became an industrial rather than an agricultural state and this tendency also had an effect on the old commons.

Bristol

Besides having many houses of colonial architecture under its elms, Bristol has a common set aside in 1781 for the use of its citizens. It is now a park and athletic field.

Little Compton

Here the village has covered most of the old common, set aside by the proprietors in 1677, with the exception of the graveyard, where there are many historic stones. Old churches, the town hall, school, and library make the common a modern as well as an ancient center for the town.

Mount Hope Farm

The site of a different sort of village from any we have considered is at Mount Hope Farm, overlooking Mount Hope Bay. Here King Philip, whose name brought terror to so many New England towns, had his village. The stones, placed to make a chair, from which he used to speak to his warriors, are still at the top of the mount. Not far away a granite marker indicates the place where he was killed.

Newport (Illustrated)

In the center of the old town of Newport is Washington Square, actually a triangle, with a bandstand and a statue of Commodore Oliver Hazard Perry. The Old Stone Mill in Touro Park—which is rather like a green—is supposed to be a tower built by the Norsemen, but was probably, in spite of this romantic legend, only a mill.

Providence (Illustrated, 2)

The First Baptist Meetinghouse, with a particularly beautiful steeple, has broad green lawns around it and despite its city setting the look of a church on some quiet country common.

The Old State House is a brick building with a tree-shaded lawn in front. It was built in 1762 and in it Rhode Island declared itself independent of England two months before the Declaration of Independence was signed in Philadelphia.

The Mall in Exchange Place is a pleasant green space in the center of the busiest part of the city. The Civil War Soldiers and Sailors Monument, designed by Randolph Rogers, is here and also a Spanish War Monument by Theo Ruggles Kitson.

Slatersville

The common, the Congregational Church, the elms, and the old houses on Green Street suggest quiet Connecticut greens, but this pattern has been applied here to an industrial settlement and is a demonstration of how well the green adapts itself to another sort of life than that of an agricultural community.

Westerley

This busy manufacturing city is centered around a spacious green called Wilcox Park. Resort hotels near by attract many summer visitors and make them more comfortable than the inn at Westerley did our friend Madam Knight on that famous journey of hers in 1704 between village greens. On her way to New Haven she stopped at Westerley at a house near the ford:

The clapboards of the house were so much asunder the light came through everywhere; the doore tyed with a cord in ye place of hinges; the floor the bear earth; nor any furniture but a bed with a glass bottle hanging at ye head on't; an earthen cup . . . a box with sticks to stand on instead of a table; and a block or two in ye corner instead of chairs . . .

Wickford

Laid out as a real estate development in 1709, Wickford seems to have profited by the enterprise. It is said to have more eighteenth-century houses than any New England village of comparable size and age.

MASSACHUSETTS

In this state there are more greens and commons than anywhere else in New England.

Amherst

> The quiet charm of Amherst Green is enhanced by the presence of two colleges—Amherst and Massachusetts State.

Andover

> The green lawns and the buildings of Phillips Andover Academy are the chief beauties of the town.

Ashby (Illustrated)

> The meetinghouse on this green carries on the architectural tradition which is Sir Christopher Wren's gift to America, as well as to England.

Auburn

> A suburb of Worcester, Auburn has a wide view from its common over the country west of Boston.

Bedford (Illustrated)

> An Indian trading post before 1640, Bedford is now a trim and prosperous settlement with a church of unusual design. In the sky above its spire great planes bound for Europe may often be seen rising from the field of the Bedford airport.

Billerica (Illustrated)

> Like all seventeenth-century settlements, Billerica developed slowly and with hardship from an outpost in the wilderness to a neat white village around the old common.

Boston (Illustrated, 6)

After more than three centuries the Common is still the heart of Boston.

The Public Garden, a continuation of the Common, is a Victorian survival where statues, flower beds, and swan boats all belong to the nineteenth century.

Louisburg Square, though owned by the proprietors whose red brick houses surround it, has the essential neighborliness of a village green.

Brewster (Illustrated)

This old Cape Cod town has been the background of many stories by Joseph C. Lincoln.

Brookfield

Like other towns in this region west of Boston, Brookfield knew the dread of Indian warfare. The town was "attacked by Indians in 1675. One garrison house defended to the last. Re-occupied twelve years later."

Brookline

A green flatiron-shaped common was a training ground for Revolutionary soldiers. With one exception, every man in town gathered there on the morning of the nineteenth of April, 1775, and went to fight at Lexington. The man who did not go was not a Tory. He explained that he just couldn't get ready in time. Here is the only green we know where there is a wishing stone. In a great mass of Roxbury pudding stone is a small red stone the color of sealing wax and the size of a thumbnail. Five generations of our family have used it with good results.

[245]

56. CAMBRIDGE, MASSACHUSETTS. Men have trained here for every war in which the country has engaged.

Boxford

Near the quiet green with its old meetinghouse, a woman accused of murder was subjected to ordeal by touch. This was probably the only occasion when the superstition that the wounds of the murdered person would bleed at the touch of the murderer was given legal standing in New England.

Byfield

Governor Dummer's old mansion here is supposed to be haunted.

Cambridge (Illustrated)

On what is known as "Cow Common" because it was a grazing field, George Washington took command of the Continental Army in 1775. The Great Elm under which he stood was one of the sights of our childhood. It was blown down some years ago and a bronze plaque marks the spot where it grew. Christ Church across from the common was used as a barracks during the Revolution. Many of the early settlers of Cambridge and eight presidents of Harvard College are buried in the graveyard near the church. On the common, the Civil War monument—an elaborate structure with a typical statue at the top of a soldier leaning on his gun—towers above the trees. Men have drilled here for every war in which the country has taken part, including World War II.

Chelmsford

A busy intersection of main roads is made pleasant by an old common and meetinghouse.

Cohasset (Illustrated)

The most beautiful of greens by the sea includes a pool, great elms, and shining white buildings.

Concord (Illustrated, 2)

Facing Monument Square are two old hostelries, the Wright Tavern and the Colonial Inn. One of the loveliest of New England churches, a graveyard with interesting inscriptions, a country store that combines the old-fashioned and the modern are also near this common to which thousands of visitors come every year because of the literary and historical traditions of the town.

Dedham

Eighteenth-century houses face a wide common, spacious enough to be undisturbed by the traffic that passes by it. Nearer the center of the town is Church Green on which is a stone placed in 1766 to honor William Pitt for his opposition to the Stamp Act. This is an unusually early memorial. The oldest frame house in America, the Fairbanks House built in 1636, is still standing in Dedham.

Deerfield (Illustrated)

That Deerfield was laid out on the common-land system we see by the offer to the Rev. John Williams of "sixteen cow commons of meadowland," if he would settle there after the massacre by King Philip's Indians had left the houses of the town empty or in ashes. With its long street of old houses, Deerfield is one of the New England towns in which one most easily steps back into the distant past. The dangers of life in such remote frontier villages is well described in *The Redeemed Captive* by the Rev. John Williams, who was carried off to Canada but returned safely.

Duxbury

Miles Standish and John Alden settled here because there was space for their cattle.

Falmouth (Illustrated)

The square houses are so near to the sea that in the War of 1812 watchers on the captains' walks could see a British ship being captured by the Americans.

Framingham (Illustrated)

In the eighteenth century this busy town was still a frontier outpost. When the road at last reached it, the opinion was that it would be sufficient for all time as no one would penetrate farther west into the wilderness.

Grafton

The common is so typical of New England greens at their best that it was chosen as the setting for the motion picture version of Eugene O'Neill's *Ah, Wilderness!*

Groton

The tones of a Paul Revere bell may be heard on this quiet common where the men who marched to Lexington gathered on the nineteenth of April, 1775.

Hardwick (Illustrated)

The town hall here with its pillared portico and short spire looks rather like an old church. A Civil War soldier leans on his musket, and the water from a memorial fountain adds to the peaceful effect of this common in the hills.

Harvard

A shady well-kept common exists in a community of much interest: Fruitlands where Bronson Alcott carried on his socialistic experiment, museums where Shaker and Indian relics may be seen, a library that houses a book collection begun by Emerson's grandfather in 1793.

Haverhill

Hannah Dustin's statue on the small triangular green recalls a woman who was captured by Indians but killed them and returned with their scalps as proof of her story. Thoreau describes her journey home with another woman and a young boy:

An Indian lurks behind every rock and pine, and their nerves cannot bear the tapping of a woodpecker—they do not stop to cook their meals upon the bank, nor land, except to carry their canoe about the falls—the ice is floating in the river— deer gaze at them from the bank—the fish hawk sails and screams overhead, and geese fly over with a startling clangor ...

Hingham

The only seventeenth-century meetinghouse still standing in New England is Hingham's Old Ship Church. South Hingham's main street has a wide green mall that runs for miles and is bordered by many eighteenth- and early nineteenth-century houses, most of them painted white but built in a variety of architectural styles.

Ipswich (Illustrated)

This town has two greens—the North and the South greens—with beautiful old buildings near both of them.

Lawrence

In this industrial city the common surrounded by public buildings is still the center.

Leominster

An old town, now a city, keeps its central common. There is also another and larger common once used as a training field for soldiers.

Lexington (Illustrated, 2)

The most famous green triangle in New England is Lexington's Battle Green. Buildings that looked out on the events of the nineteenth of April, 1775, are little changed.

Longmeadow

Settled in 1644 on a "long meddowe" bought from the Indians, the town is famous for the spacious beauty of its green mall with its wide lawns and great trees.

Martha's Vineyard

At Oak Bluffs on this island an unusual community, first composed of tents and later of small Gothic cottages, has grown up around a Methodist Tabernacle on a green, shaded by oaks.

Nahant

This pleasant summer resort, known as "Cold Roast Boston" was once a pasture for the cattle of the citizens of Lynn. It was bought from an Indian chief for a suit, two stone pestles, and a jew's-harp.

Nantucket (Illustrated)

Stretches of moorland on this island are still called the commons. Wills of Nantucket citizens used to bequeath shares in cow commons and sheep commons to their heirs. Town Square is the center of the town but now no grass grows there unless it can push up between the cobblestones.

Newburyport

There are several restful green spaces in this old seaport—among them Bartlett Mall and Brown's Park—and many fine mansions of the Federal period.

North Andover

Near the common is the Kittredge Memorial honoring many generations of physicians in one family.

North Carver

On the green is the site of King Philip's Spring where Indians, returning from a raid in 1675, stopped to wash the blood of victims from their hands.

Pittsfield

The original village green is now City Hall Park. Soldiers were mustered and trained here. In 1810 the first cattle show in America was held here. A sundial marks the spot where stood a famous elm, which fell at the age of almost three centuries.

Plymouth (Illustrated)

The oldest permanent settlement in New England was begun on the principle of goods as well as land owned in common. The monument on the training green is unusual in being surmounted by an eagle.

Quincy

At Mount Wollaston, once part of Quincy, Thomas Morton set up a maypole on the green and taught Indians to dance around it to the horror of his Puritan neighbors.

Rowley

The energetic citizens of this town built a ninety-ton ship on the common and with a hundred yoke of oxen dragged it to the river more than a mile away. To celebrate the launching, a barrel of rum was poured into a well and the guests helped themselves.

Royalston (Illustrated)

A sleepy, unspoiled hilltop common has near it some exceptionally fine houses of the square, hip-roofed type.

Salem (Illustrated)

On the eight acres of Washington Square face handsome brick houses, some of them designed by Samuel McIntire.

South Hadley

This is a college town which owes much of its beauty to the campus of Mount Holyoke College. (The campuses of Smith College at Northampton and of Williams at Williamstown also add to the attractiveness of the towns they occupy.)

Springfield

In this town is a settlement known as Storrowton. It contains a group of old buildings bought and placed around a central green through the generosity of Mrs. James Jackson Storrow. Perhaps even better than existing New England villages, Storrowton shows how towns used to look. It includes a meetinghouse, a little red schoolhouse, dwellings, and a tavern.

Sturbridge (Illustrated)

Here is a wide shady common with an old tavern facing it.

Some distance away is Old Sturbridge Village. This is the hobby of Albert B. Wells of Southbridge, who has had old buildings transported to a tract of land in Sturbridge and arranged there around a common. A country store, blacksmith's shop, cabinetmaker's shop, shoe shop, and old houses are part of this new-old village where craftsmen actually work at their trades and pass on their knowledge to younger men.

57. WENHAM, MASSACHUSETTS: The meetinghouse is the center of a town from which ice was shipped to India.

Taunton

On the green is the General Cobb Boulder marking an event in Shay's Rebellion when General Cobb dispersed a mob there.

Templeton (Illustrated)

A quiet hill town with an especially beautiful old meetinghouse on the green.

Topsfield

There are seventeenth-century houses near the green of this lovely, unspoiled town.

Wayland (Illustrated)

The Unitarian Church suggests the work of Sir Christopher Wren and is unusual in having a long and decorative line of horse sheds still standing beside it.

Webster

Old cannon mark the common of this industrial town where the handsome new town hall is designed in the spirit of earlier buildings.

Wenham (Illustrated)

The First Church was founded here in 1644; the present building was erected in 1843. There are seventeenth- and eighteenth-century houses near it. This town had an unusual connection with the Orient. Ice used to be cut on Wenham Lake and carried to India on clipper ships. One of Kipling's stories in *The Jungle Book* tells about a crane that swallowed a lump of ice from Wenham Lake. Like the crane, the people in India were astounded at having the ice disappear and leave them with nothing. The first captains of the ships that carried the ice were instructed to give it away, until people acquired a taste for it.

West Boylston

A peaceful common with an old graveyard near it.

West Bridgewater

The town still holds the deed given by Massasoit
when he sold the land on which it stands for thirty
dollars' worth of merchandise.

West Newbury (Illustrated)

The village pump stands on a common with compact,
comfortable New England houses facing it.

Wrentham (Illustrated)

This town, once part of Dedham, was burned by
the Indians in King Philip's War. A granite stone
marks the site of the meetinghouse of 1684. The
present meetinghouse suffered damage in the hurri-
cane of 1938 when the beautiful spire was destroyed.
Fortunately the original plans were found and the
spire has been carefully restored.

NEW HAMPSHIRE

The pattern of New Hampshire towns is often that of a
main street or a crossroads, but there are some old commons
well worth seeing, if only we can draw our gaze long enough
from the mountains, lakes, and rivers of this beautiful state.

Charlestown

Six log houses with a log fort were the beginning of
this town known as "No. 4" because it was the
fourth in a chain of frontier outposts. The very wide
main street was once a common where soldiers drilled.

Chester (Illustrated)

A white church of nineteenth-century architecture, lovely arching elms, old cannon, and a granite monument with a figure in Civil War uniform calmly surveying the village make this a typical green in the hills. It was from Chester that Lord Timothy Dexter went to Newburyport in search of a suitably fashionable background.

Exeter

Dignified eighteenth-century houses with beautifully executed dentil cornices and handsome doorways stand in the shade of great elms. One of the oldest buildings in the state, the Garrison House, built in 1650, is here. It has small windows, almost like loopholes, and a door that once had a portcullis to be raised in time of danger. Close by is Hemlock Square where troops drilled in the seventeenth century. Its name came from the custom of throwing hemlock boughs on the ground in wet weather to prevent the soldiers from getting stuck in the mud.

Fitzwilliam (Illustrated)

The neatly fenced common is especially pleasant in autumn.

Hancock (Illustrated)

Meetinghouse, tavern, houses, and bandstand make this one of the most attractive of New Hampshire greens.

Hanover (Illustrated)

The union of college and town is a beautiful example of good town planning.

Haverhill Corner

The common here belongs to the proprietors whose fine houses face it.

Hill

The new town built here when the old one was put out of existence by a flood-control project, follows a New England idea of town planning. Neighbors wished to remain together, so a new site was selected to which some houses were moved bodily. Others were rebuilt there. The new town hall faces a spacious common with a pool. The stores, filling station, and the small factory that is the town's only industry are all attractive white buildings with a neat and prosperous air. With traffic diverted from the main street, the new town is pleasanter than the old one.

Hillsborough Center

Here the common is stone-walled and there is a pond to increase its peaceful appearance.

Kingston

The wide lawns of the houses grouped around this large common produce a spacious effect.

Lebanon (Illustrated)

Even the factory on the corner of this restful shady common is a neat well-kept building.

Lisbon

Built around the site of a blockhouse and a stockade, Lisbon has seen transportation change from oxcart to airplane and its meadows from cornfields, hoed by Indian squaws, to landing fields. The first town meeting was held in 1790 in the blockhouse, which is now part of the Cobleigh Tavern.

Lyme (Illustrated)

This is one of the loveliest of New Hampshire's
Connecticut River villages with a distinguished
church spire dominating the green.

Nottingham Square

The common is wide, fine old houses frame it, and
there is a far view over the southeastern part of the
state.

Orford (Illustrated)

Washington Irving called this the most beautiful village he had ever seen. Time has done nothing to
change its loveliness.

Plaistow

Shrubbery has been planted about this well-kept
green. Piled cannon balls around the monument are
always freshly painted and look as slick and shining
as the stove of a New England housekeeper.

Portsmouth

Along Middle Street and in the region of Hay-
market Square—hay was sold here in 1755—are
some of the most beautiful houses not only in New
England but anywhere in the country. The Peirce
House, a three-storied mansion of the Federal period with wonderfully carved woodwork, is open to
the public.

Rindge (Illustrated)

There is an especially fine meetinghouse set on a
breezy common among the hills.

Rochester

The common has been the center of the town since
1780.

Sandown

A meetinghouse with exceptionally fine woodwork was built here in 1775.

South Sutton (Illustrated)

On Old Home Day when neighbors, wearing their ancestors' clothing, drive to church, the meetinghouse looks as it must have in the nineteenth century.

Troy

Here the common is surrounded by a fence, as many greens were in the early days.

Warren

This pleasant green delights every traveler.

Wentworth

The common here preserves the charm of an earlier day.

Winchester

The town is divided by the Ashuelot River. There is a small common on the east side of the river.

MAINE

In Maine, perhaps the most interesting green is on Indian Island—off Old Town in the Penobscot River—where a monument stands in memory of Penobscot Indians killed in the Revolution. Inscribed on the stone are the names of Indians who fought in the Continental Army.

There are, of course, attractive parks in many Maine towns and these take the place of village greens in other states. In Coburn Park in Skowhegan a boulder marks the site of Benedict Arnold's camp. Bradley Memorial Park in

Fryeburg is the place chosen for the soldiers' monument. Bethel has an elm-shaded quadrangular park. Orono, like other New England college towns, is beautified by the campus of the University of Maine. Bates College brings ivy-covered walls and green shade, in the manner of a common, to the industrial city of Lewiston.

In Augusta, the twenty-acre State Park in front of the Capitol is the place where Maine regiments camped in the Civil War. At Fort Western, an old garrison house has been restored and appropriately furnished and block houses and palisades have been reproduced. The first settlement in this region, a fur trading post of Plymouth Colony, was established here.

Alfred and Union are Maine towns with pleasant green commons.

Bath (Illustrated)

Here is a parklike green still much enjoyed as a recreation spot with its pond and fountain.

Wiscasset (Illustrated, 2)

On the beautiful sloping common here the Marie Antoinette House was once prepared by Captain Clough's wife to receive the ill-fated queen. Many handsome buildings face this green.

VERMONT

The greens of this state are all the lovelier for their impressive mountain settings.

Addison

This town looks out on the Adirondacks and on Lake Champlain. The green is fenced in and the memorial of World War I has a machine gun mounted on it.

Barre

The busy main street opens out into a green space with a heroic-sized male figure cut in Barre granite. It symbolizes "Youth Victorious" with determination expressed in the steadily held sword and humility in the kneeling posture.

Bennington (Illustrated)

This first town west of the Connecticut River to be given a grant has one of Vermont's most beautiful churches. It stands near the battlefield of the Revolution.

Bradford

The green here is narrow with a statue of Admiral Clark on it. The only New England state with no seacoast produced two of the country's small number of full admirals—Charles Edgar Clark and George Dewey.

Brattleboro

One New Year's morning a snow angel once appeared on the small triangular green here.

Bristol (Illustrated)

The church on the green lifts up a spire silhouetted by the hills.

Burlington

There are several expanses of green in this lakeside city. College Green, the campus of the University of Vermont, is one of them. Battery Park with its background of mountains and lake is another. However, what most impresses the visitor are the wide lawns with their arching rows of elms between sidewalk and street. Seen from the lake, the whole city is a green.

58. Bristol, Vermont. The church lifts up its spire towards the hills.

Checkerberry Village

Around Checkerberry Green is a group of small primitive houses near the Lamoille River. The settlement, away from main roads, looks much as it did when Ethan Allen came through this part of Vermont.

Chelsea

Two maple-shaded commons parallel each other on sloping ground.

Craftsbury Common (Illustrated)

This daughter town of Sturbridge, Massachusetts, occupies a high plateau beautified by well-kept lawns and flower gardens and immaculate white houses, and with wide views of the Green Mountains.

Danville Green

The common has a bandstand and a Civil War monument.

Fairhaven

Here is another spacious, white-fenced common.

Guildhall

The center of the town is a grassy quadrangle surrounded by pleasant houses and public buildings.

Lyndonville (Illustrated)

In a world dominated by motor traffic, people on Lyndonville's common enjoy watching a trotting race in the snow.

Manchester

White marble sidewalks edge beautifully trimmed lawns so wide the main street looks like a village green. Actually the green itself is long and narrow.

59. LYNDONVILLE, VERMONT. Horse races are a gay sight along this
snug common.

A figure in the uniform of a Revolutionary soldier honors Vermonters who fought for American independence.

Middlebury

A well-kept common forms the center of the town. The Congregational Church, similar to the one at Bennington, was also built by Lavius Fillmore.

Montpelier

Here the green is a velvety, open, elm-shaded space stretching out in front of the State Capitol.

Newbury

The green is a long rectangle close to the region where the Connecticut River opens up to make wide oxbows among rich fields.

Newfane

There are two greens here—a wide common from which Newfane volunteers went forth to fight in the battle of Bennington and a shady green surrounded by fine public buildings. We have been told there are so few lawbreakers in Newfane that the town rents out space in the jail to tourists, but that may be only a rumor.

Rutland

The green on Main Street is a slender oblong, so long it is almost a mall.

St. Albans

Here the central common is known as Taylor Park.

St. Johnsbury

The shady green is called Arnold Park. The Civil War Monument by Larkin Goldsmith Mead is in Court House Square.

Shelburne

The town center is an oval green faced by well-designed modern buildings.

Thetford Hill (Illustrated)

An old academy, a white meetinghouse, and pleasant houses border this irregularly shaped, quiet common.

Weston (Illustrated)

A fenced-in circular green is the center of a town in which old-time industries, newly revived, are bringing prosperity and a satisfying community life.

Whitingham

The common here is still used as a place of recreation.

Woodstock

Lovely old houses of white clapboards, rose-pink brick, mellow ivory or amber stone face a narrow green ellipse. The town was once known as Woodstock Green or simply The Green and has good right to this distinction.

We asked a friend to tell us something about the common in her village.

"Why," she replied, "it's—it's just a common."

And so it proved to be. It is not especially large nor particularly beautiful. No stirring events took place there and it does not have the highest church spire nor the oldest elms. It is simply a pleasant open space in a town with one or two busy streets. There are homelike houses near it and a Civil War Monument as ugly as plenty of others. The grass needs a good deal of expensive treatment and the fence could do with a coat of paint. The inhabitants of the town take the common for granted, but if anyone seriously suggested selling it for building lots, the same inhabitants would bring out the first tar and feathers seen in these parts since Skipper Ireson's ride.

Whether a green is large and busy like Boston Common or quietly peaceful like Litchfield's lovely place; whether history was made there as at Lexington, or romance hovers over it as at Wiscasset; whether the men who crossed it sailed to the Orient as at Salem, or with guns over their shoulders herded cattle as at Billerica; whether its beauty lies in fine houses beautifully placed like Orford's, in compact neatness as at Ipswich, or in a wonderful location as on Craftsbury Common's airy plateau—wherever it is and however it looks, New England roots go as deep down into it as those of the great trees that shade it.

Hawthorne remarked that, "No man who needs a monument ever ought to have one."

The village greens of New England are a memorial to the courage, vision, and self-sacrifice of men and women who have—and need—no other monument.

Index

Nantucket town—*continued*
  Town Square, 152, 154-155
    illus., 153
  whaling, 154
Napoleon, 93, 174
Needham, Massachusetts, 116, 139-140
New England characteristics, 227-233
New Hampshire, 24, 181-198
  claim to Vermont territory, 202
  inns, 58
  list of greens, 256-260
New Haven, Connecticut, 26, 177-180
  Proprietors' Committee, 177, 180
  planting of elms, 178
  green as civic center, 178-180, 239
    illus., 179
New Orleans, battle of, 132
New York State, 55
  claim to part of Vermont, 202
Newbury, Vermont, 200, 266
  rectangular common, 200-201
Newburyport, Massachusetts, 91, 93-94, 162, 251
Newfane, Vermont, 266
Newport, Rhode Island, 157-160, 163, 242
  common, 193
  Old Stone Mill, 242
  Touro Park, *illus.,* 158
Norsemen, 159-160
North Andover, Massachusetts, 252
North Carver, Massachusetts, 252
Northampton, Massachusetts, 198
Norway Pond, 193
Norwood, Massachusetts, 26
Nottingham Square, New Hampshire, 259

Oak Bluffs, Martha's Vineyard, 155-157
Old Burying Ground, Bennington, Vermont, 202
Old Burying Ground, Hall's Corner, 147
Old Burying Ground, Temple, New Hampshire, 188
Old Congregational Church, Thetford Hill, 198
Old Connecticut Path, 182
Old Elm, Boston Common, 127, 134
Old Granary Burying Ground, 123
Old Hill Burying Ground, Newburyport, 94

Old Lyme, Connecticut, 239
Old Ship Church, Hingham, Massachusetts, 43, 250
Old State House, Providence, 163
  illus., 164
Old Stone Mill, Newport, 159-160
  illus., 158
Old Sturbridge Village, 253
O'Neill, Eugene, *Ah, Wilderness!* 26, 249
Orange County Court House, Chelsea, Vermont, 201
Orchard House, Concord, 67
Ordeal by touch, 247
Orford, New Hampshire, 81-84, 259
  illus., 83
Orono, Maine, 261
Orton, Vrest, rebuilding of village pattern, 215
Oxbow Antique Shop, 201

Pacific Ocean, 152, 232
Palladian windows, 75, 88, 202
"Paradise," Smith College, Northampton, 198
Park Street Church, Boston, 106, 123
  steeple, *illus.,* 37
Parker, Captain John, 115, 117, 118
Parker, Theodore, quoted, 115-116
Parker House, Boston, 123
Passaconway, sachem, 104
Patty and Polly, 61
Peirce House, Portsmouth, New Hampshire, 259
Peirce-Nichols House, Salem, 77-78
Pepys, Samuel, 128
Percy, Lord, quoted on Lexington battle, 117-118
Perry, Commodore Oliver Hazard, 132, 242
Philip, King, *see* King Philip's War
Philips, Henry, 128
Phillips, Wendell, quoted, 132-133
Phyllis, cook, 163
Pickle for the Knowing Ones, 94
Pies, 224
Pingree House, Salem, 78
Pitcairn, Major, 63, 115-117, 182
Pitt, William, 248
Pittsfield, Massachusetts, 252
Plains of Abraham, 118
Plaistow, New Hampshire, 259
Plum Island, 97

[276]